# Architect of Smiles

# Architect of Smiles

Pat Foy, DDS

To Rebecca & Scott:
Thanks for your support
& been threatening to
write this! Hope you
enjoy it
Pat Foy DDS

Grateful acknowledgement is extended to the publications where some of these stories originally appeared: "A Class I Missed In Dental School," *Nothwest Dentistry* and *ADA News*; "Grandmother's Kitchen," *South Dakota Magazine*. I would also like to acknowledge the late Georgia Gould, who was my editor and cheerleader, and John Toren, who help me to finalize and produce the book. But I have to give my family top billing for allowing me to hunker down in the basement on crappy-weather days, so I could pound out these stories. To one and all, many thanks! – Pat Foy, DDS



Although the stories in this book are true, names and details have sometimes been changed to protect the privacy of those involved.

*to my wife Lynne and daughters*
*Sarah and Katherine—they have put*
*up with my storytelling for*
*many, many years.*

# Contents

# Architect of Smiles

# Learning, In and Out of School

## Code Blue Room 708

*"Do not dwell on the past; do not dream of the future, concentrate the mind on the present moment."*

– Buddha

My brain was in a fuzzy fog and my body seemed bound to the bed when I emerged from sleep to a loud, metallic clanging and a monstrous, racking cough.

*Where am I?* I asked myself. It dawned on me eventually that I was lying in a metal hospital bed, held down by stiff, white sheets. I tried to loosen their smothering grip, but the instant I began to move my arms and legs a jabbing pain hit my gut along with the memory of an angry appendix.

The coughing stopped and the rattling ceased. Rain hit the windows; thunder grumbled in the distance. I felt weary and confused. I had recently arrived at the University of Nebraska in Lincoln to pursue my dental studies. Every emotion from excited confidence to sheer terror had been part of my two-week initiation. Earlier that day, a stern, middle-aged doctor had told me, "Yes, I believe it is your appendix, but we won't know for certain until we get in there. Have you contacted your folks?"

Presuming I'd make a quick recovery, I replied: "No, I don't want to bother them, I'll be out in a couple of days."

"Son," he said, "you may die on the table."

That verbal slap in the face was my first taste of personal mortality.

Suddenly, as I hazily reviewed the chain of events that had brought me to this situation, a swollen bladder seized my attention. I couldn't find a button for the nurse in the dark, so I quickly tried to crawl out before I wet the bed. My bare feet hit the cold floor and cold air hit my bare back, but it was impossible to stand up straight without excruciating pain. Humped over, I went creeping to find the restroom.

The man in the next bed snored and gasped for air. Nearby, a small woman seemed to be asleep, curled up on a makeshift recliner.

As I lifted up my hospital gown to commence my blessed relief, I was shocked to see they had shaved me. Someone had touched my private parts without my permission! I felt violated until it occurred to me that they needed a sterile field for my surgery. I had no cause for complaint.

By the time I began to hunch back to bed, the pain from walking was already less intense. The a soft light from the restroom fell on the woman in the chair and as I passed she lifted her head. Her face was unadorned and she had short, curly-brown hair. She appeared to be about fifty.

The man kept desperately gasping for air. His shadow showed an enormous, obese body and I was struck suddenly by the fact that this guy might be dying. This realization called to mind a hospital visit I'd made at the age of fourteen when my grandmother was dying from lung cancer. All my fondest memories of the times we'd spent together were erased by the horrific images of her last beleaguered breaths, as she thrashed about and recounted a succession of tormented memories. Her death did not appear to be unduly painful, but it was definitely emotionally charged. I still resent the fact that my parents allowed me to witness this scene, but it did enforce the understanding that death is something real.

All this seemed relevant as I inched my way back to the bed. I did not want to experience the pain he was going through. In the course of the night, his incessantly struggles for air became so commonplace that only an unusually violent gasp would attract my attention.

The next morning was Saturday. I woke to gray, overcast skies and a nurse's sullen, nasal voice as she interrogated my neighbor behind a closed curtain.

Suddenly, she jerked back the curtain and honked over at me, "Good Morning, Trooper! Welcome to Room 708. My name is Jo and if you need me, buzz anytime." She pointed to the two-way intercom attached to my bed rail and sailed out of the room.

I was still trying to adjust to the murky daylight when I spotted my roommate's upper torso. His open gown exposed a huge wound spreading across a massive, shaved chest. It was stapled shut and weeping with pus, blood and air bubbles. The man appeared to be in his mid-fifties with a full head of black hair, graying at the temples. His weathered face was scarred from adolescent acne, but his square jaw and dominant nose projected wisdom and strength.

His soft, manly voice whispered, "Hello, I'm Tom Richert, and this is my wife, Jerry."

"I'm Pat, and I'm pleased to meet the two of you."

He chuckled. "You may not be after you get to know us." He looked at his wife with a loving smile. I did not know what he meant and was left curious.

At that point, introductions having been concluded, the two of them started up a conversation as if I weren't present. His wife insisted that he rest and not see his visitors. He replied that if they'd taken the trouble to come, he was obliged to see them. The argument which ensued, interrupted by fits of coughing, continued for quite a while. Reviewing their schedule, the woman informed her husband that she would be gone for a time at the end of the day to attend to their two teenage daughters.

My first hospital meal consisted of a clear, boring liquid which Tom and I ate together while his wife went to the cafeteria. As we began to chat he struck me as a pleasant and respectable individual, though his eyes were haggard and his skin seemed slightly jaundiced. In the course of our conversation I learned that for many years he'd been a dispatcher for the Lincoln Police Department. He'd known for some time that there was something wrong with his health, but, being a typical male, he ignored it as long as possible. His habit of smoking had taken its toll, and he was diagnosed with lung cancer. Although they attempted to remove the cancer surgically, it was deemed "inoperable."

I told him a little about myself, my career plans, and my family back in Sioux City.

The rest of the day was taken up with visits and phone calls. My parents arrived before noon, and once they realized I was fine, they went home to fulfill a previous commitment.

Tom spent most of the day with friends in the waiting room, returning to his bed only occasionally for a short rest which was invariably interrupted by fits of coughing and gasping for breath.

I tried not to stare at him while he slept, but I couldn't help watch the battle going on in his chest. His wife remained in the room as he napped. I assumed she didn't want him to die alone. For myself, haunted by images of my grandmother's final moments, I loathed the thought of being present when he died and was determined to get out of here as fast as possible.

I had planned on doing some studying while recuperating, but the pain medications I was taking dragged my comprehension level to near zero, so I quit taking them. I hoped that going cold turkey would also speed up my release. I just wanted to go home.

That evening I was able to eat anything I wanted. My plumbing was in good working order and I could walk almost entirely upright. Visiting hours were over and Tom's parade of visitors had come to an end. He was finally able to lie down in peace. Mrs. Richert had left to attend to the kids.

Tom closed his eyes and quickly nodded off. The hospital floor seemed very peaceful, but as the lights dimmed for the evening, I felt a kind of emptiness.

The nurse checked in and asked me if there was anything I needed. "No, I'm okay, but thanks for asking."

She seemed to sense something and asked if I'd like a back rub. It was the just the touch I was longing for. Her warm hands soothed my fears and loneliness. She smelled like lilacs.

"How is your incision?" she asked.

"The surgeon gave me a bikini cut."

She chuckled, "So, you wear bikinis?"

"No, no, but it was a small cut." I was trying to preserve my masculinity.

"I see you haven't had anything for pain since your surgery. You don't need to suffer, you know."

"Yeh, I know, but I just want to get out of this place." I nodded at my sleeping neighbor.

She whispered, "I don't blame you." Then off she went, leaving her lilacs behind.

All of a sudden I heard a loud gasp. Tom was wheezing, choking, taking deep-extended breaths. His jerking body rattled the bed louder than ever. Should I call the nurse? The noises were so eerie, I dreaded the end.

He finally reduced his huffing and puffing, caught his breath, and calmly asked, "How's it going?"

I was enormously relieved that he was still alive. "I'm doing great. I've completed studying for my Monday exams and hope to get out tomorrow."

He replied, "I envy you. You have your whole life ahead of you. You're young and I know you'll be a great dentist. Here I am about to die and I barely understand what the hell my life was all about."

I sensed he had already processed his imminent death in one way or another, grieved for himself, and now he was preparing for the final chapter.

He continued, "You know, when I was in high school I was not much interested in school work. I had no goals for myself and did enough just to get by. All I wanted was my freedom from the school system and to get out of my parents' loveless home."

Pausing to breathe, his face was contorted in physical and mental pain. "I had no idea at the time that an education would have given me more choices in life."

"When I graduated from high school, the Korean War was underway, and I joined the military along with all of my other buddies who didn't know what to do.

"The Army told me I had an aptitude for the Military Police, so I let the service choose my career. In my typical way, I was overly obedient and too compliant; I never questioned myself about my own personal wishes. I really never, never thought about my personal passions for a career. I was such a fool."

He lowered his head as if he were ashamed. The silence was deafening as he lay there with his eyes closed.

My impulse was to comfort him. I searched for the right words, if only to break the painful silence. "Only God knows."

"God knows," he repeated. He looked up at the ceiling as if he were searching for God. "I've never been a religious man. I witnessed guys in Korea who died peacefully because of their faith in a God. They seemed to be called by Him."

He continued to stare off into space. "My wife's God has

comforted her. She was able to introduce me to Him, and I hope He will understand me." His eyes roved aimlessly across the ceiling as if he were searching the heavens.

"After the Korean war, I came back to Lincoln and joined the police force. I never stretched my mind, my skills or my talents. I was too contented as a cop. I never questioned myself. I never questioned what I really wanted to do with my life. It was just the easy way. I always took the path of least resistance. I was such a damn compliant kid, so the police department seemed to fit my stupid ass."

He sat up in bed and turned to me with life burning fire in his eyes, "Never get goddamn compliant. Question yourself. Question your superiors. Question your life."

Tom's words were confirming a part of my being that was already there. My father, through both his words and his actions, he taught me a healthy disrespect for authority. He never put humans up on a pedestal due to their profession or social standing, not priests or presidents or popes. Parochial schools had caused me some grief, but now I was thankful for my father's wisdom.

"Time on the police force passed by, and all of my cop friends started to get married. 'The boys' seemed more important than anyone else at that time. So, even though I didn't love my wife, we got married. She was actually my social ticket and we lived together in a loveless relationship." He shook his head regretfully. You'd think I would have learned something from my parents."

I could see his pain reflecting from his eyes.

"My wife wanted to have kids; I suppose she was lonely. I really wasn't there for her or the girls. I never understood how to be present for others." He was choking out his words as he spoke, writhing sporadically in pain. He seemed to be sinking to a new low.

"The Police Department promoted me to dispatcher, and that's what I did for the rest of my life."

This confession of a wasted, empty life was moving, and I reached for the right words. "I'll bet you saved lives in Korea and on the force."

Yeh, but that was my job"

"But you saved lives."

"Just doing my job."

"Not everyone saves a life."

"I could not save them all." His eyes swelled with rage, and he looked away. "Goddamn it, if I was doing my job, they wouldn't have destroyed Randy."

"Randy?"

"Over in Korea, Randy and I were on duty at the brig when a bunch of intoxicated officers came over after a night on the town. They came to spring one of their pompous officer buddies. I was too damn intimidated by the brass, but Randy knew we had the authority to stop them. I didn't dare. He fought back without my help and they eventually crucified him. He was not guilty of anything, but they had him court marshaled. Dishonorable discharge. I could have saved Randy, but I was stupid and scared. Randy's pride was too much. He used his own military issue to blow his head off."

My gut told me to shut up; I just hoped he would keep on talking.

"I've never questioned anything in my life and now I'm going to die. This has finally forced me to ask myself what in the hell I've been doing? I never looked into my own wants or desires. I just put my right foot in front of my left on automatic pilot. Like a hamster spinning in a wheel, I went nowhere!"

There was a long, silent pause. I remained uncomfortably quiet until I couldn't stand it. "You served your country and you served your community. You should be proud of your service."

He appeared to be staring at his feet. "Being a police dispatcher for all of those years, you don't remember all the things that went right. You never give yourself credit for safe situations. Keeping cops safe and getting EMS dispatched quickly was my job.

"But, I do remember when cops got shot after I dispatched them or when they crashed their cars. I was constantly haunted with the thought that if I had done something differently, I might have saved them.

"No, I was never proud of doing my job. I was always beating myself up for not being perfect. Then I would take it out on everyone around me. I was a bastard at times.

"In fact, I almost lost my job and my family over another woman. They hired a young female dispatcher who I was supposed to train and supervise. I was only thinking below my belt. She was a smart cookie who used me, then spit me out like an old piece of meat. The Force had to pay her a large settlement for my horny stupidity.

"My wife wasn't surprised; she took it all in stride. She probably thought it was the price she had to pay for marrying such a loveless jerk like me.

"I was a fool. But, you know, with all this cancer stuff, how she's loved and cared for me, I could finally see her true beauty. She's not a pretty woman on the outside, but she has been an angel to me and my children.

"Then, about two weeks ago it happened. I fell in love with my own wife."

He beamed a smile of joy, his tearful eyes sparkled and he began to sob. We looked at each other and said nothing until I also swelled with tears. Normally this would have embarrassed me, but instead I felt the manly love of a friend, a closeness to a fellow human being in a way I had never expected.

I was grieving for this man who only a moment ago was a complete stranger to me. He had confided his ignorance, his lack of purpose and I was honored to be the one to hear his confession.

I was sad for him and his family, but fortunate for his wisdom.

Tom panted for air and his face grew troubled. Sitting up straight he looked directly at me. "You're young, smart and full of energy. The world is out there waiting for you. You can choose whatever you want to be. Don't waste it!"

He stared deep into my being. "Make the hard choices in life. Don't look back. Don't regret things that you have no control over. Most of the time the right way is the hard way."

I realized at that moment that thus far, my life had come to me too easily, and for the first time a sense of guilt, of privilege, began to grip me. I was confused, yet I also felt, once again for the first time, a vague sense of personal responsibility. More than ever I needed to question and find a personal meaning for myself. Tom might not have lived an enviable life, but now he was leaving me the gift of his personal reality. I suddenly wondered about all those visitors. How many other lives had he touched with new awareness?

The nurse came in. "How are you doing, Mr. Richert? Is there anything I can do for you?" Tom shook his head no. His face was wet and his tormented eyes were overflowing.

"Do you need something for pain?" Again Tom shook his head negatively. She left the room with a puzzled look on her face. We looked at each other and said nothing.

Mrs. Richert returned and they exchanged small talk until he fell asleep. She prepared the chair in the corner of our room. I opened my text books, but couldn't concentrate.

That night I grew up. Tom had made me examine myself more critically than ever before. Was I living the life I should be living? Did I really want to be a dentist? Why was I dating the girl I was dating? Was I living my life just to please my parents? Would I have anything to be proud if I died tomorrow? How could I create a life that would bring me peace should I find myself in a situation similar to the one Tom was in? It was a long, tough night.

On Sunday morning the uplifting voice of a perky, new nurse woke me up. The sun was shining so brightly, I couldn't open my eyes without squinting. Our dingy, dark space seemed to glow fresh and clean. Tom was sitting up in bed. The color of his face had changed. His eyes had a new sparkle.

I, too, had an overwhelming sense of resolve. Tom had given me a new perspective on life.

Sunday in the hospital was calm. My surgeon had already written my dismissal orders and take-home medication prescriptions. Soon my college roommate arrived to pick me up.

Tom was in the restroom and we were gathering my few belongings together when Mrs. Richert came over and whispered, "This morning Tom finally seems to be at peace with himself. What did you tell him? He thinks a lot of you."

I said, "After last night, I feel like he's my second father. I did nothing but listen. He told me that he loves you and regrets he was not always able to be there for you and the girls."

Her face glowed with joy, and now I, too, could see her beauty. As she walked away and began to tidy up the room, it seemed as if she were floating.

Tom came out and said he was glad for me to be going home. When I went to shake his hand, he grabbed mine with both hands and squeezed firmly.

"Go for it! And remember to make those hard choices." He had the same loving smile from the night before.

I thanked him and went out of that room with the weight of the Tom's wisdom on my shoulders, and a lifetime ahead to see if I could put it into practice.

Mrs. Richert walked down the hall with us to the elevator. When we were out of ear shot from Tom, she called, "Pat!" I stopped, trying to hide my tears; she grabbed and hugged me.

Her clutch felt like an eternity. We were both crying, though neither of us said a word.

The elevator door opened and her two teenage daughters came out. They were speechless to see their reserved mother weeping in the arms of a strange boy.

Mrs. Richert let me go and hugged them. "These are our two girls, Jenny and Margaret. This is your father's friend, Pat, and his roommate."

Suddenly, an announcement erupted from the intercom: *"Code Blue Room 708! Code Blue Room 708!"* We turned towards Tom's room to see a flurry of nurses rushing in. Mrs. Richert ran towards them and her daughters reluctantly followed.

There was nothing more for me to do. Room 708 was no longer my place. Tom was dying and I would only be in the way.

# A Horse Taught Me Not to Pass the Buck

*Only the curious will learn and only the resolute overcome the obstacles to learning. The quest quotient has always excited me more than the intelligence quotient.*

– Eugene S. Wilson (1900-1981)
Dean of Admissions, Amherst College

My dental education did not begin with dental school; it started one summer when I was sixteen and learned to break a colt.

My father's small hobby farm in southeastern South Dakota was nestled between two rivers—the Missouri to the west and the Big Sioux to the east. The area was flat, fertile farmland, an ancient, majestic river-bottom sparsely populated with small acreages. It was an expansive training ground for my teenage discoveries, in nature and in myself.

In the summer of 1971, my project was to break a three-year-old mare named Nevelee. She was reddish brown with a black mane and a white star on her chest. I was eager but totally lacking in experience and intimidated by the size and power of this beautiful, muscular beast. My dad and I wanted to do it right, not like in the movies where a cowboy bucks a bronco into submission.

We researched horse-breaking philosophies, consulted libraries and interrogated local farmers, and in the process we came up with a wide range of techniques.

At last we met a man who had spent his lifetime raising horses. He offered me a 4-H manual on how to train a horse to be a partner on the ride. I still cherish the knowledge that led me down a trail that few people experience and taught me about my own self-control.

The manual described the process of forming a partnership with a horse step-by-step, but without insisting on a strict timetable, as every animal will respond differently. The biggest challenge for an inexperienced trainer was to recognize when the horse was ready to move onto something new.

My initial goal was to get Nevelee to like me. I began by courting her slowly, touching her back, talking in her ear, stroking her mane, patting the side of her neck—anything she might find pleasurable—until she became comfortable with my presence.

The next step was to get the horse to trust me. I began developing observational skills, applying patience with the horse and restraint for myself. The dance continued until Nevelee let me slip the bridle over her head. At first it was for only a few seconds, then for a more extended time, and finally it no longer bothered her at all. At that point, it became a game and the horse started helping me put it on.

After bridling, we started "the lead." I rode ahead on her mother, Blacky, leading Nevelee by the reins. It took time for her to permit the saddle, but she learned quickly. First I put on a blanket and waited until she got used to it. Then the saddle was placed on top, at first with a loose cinch, which was gradually tightened each time until she had no problem wearing it. The urge I felt to slip onto her back grew to the point where it was almost unbearable, but after all the time I'd spent with her, it was obvious to me she wasn't ready.

The next step was to increase the weight on the saddle, at first with one feed bag, then slowly adding more as she became more comfortable with what she was carrying. As she got more relaxed with the increasing weight I began to be cautiously optimistic that she about ready for me to mount.

On that memorable day, our routine was duplicated without incident. I slipped on the bridle, laid the blanket on her back, saddled and securely tightened the strap. My father was riding ahead on Blacky, ready to gently lead the young mare.

At first I petted and talked to her. Then I went to her left side, put my hand in the stirrup and pressed down for her to feel the pressure. I did this several times, reassuring her that it was okay. When she became calm, I put my left foot into the stirrup and waited. She seemed to tolerate it. Grabbing the saddle horn, I lifted myself up, swung my right leg over her back and started to put my boot into the second stirrup. Her rear end quivered uneasily. I tried it several times, but she clearly didn't like the pressure of my right knee on her flank. I rode lopsided that day, and she barely tolerated the load.

The training continued. I taught Nevelee the principles of reining—to turn, stop and go. My father and Blacky rode ahead, and when the distance between horses extended to twenty feet, it was time to eliminate the lead.

For months, I had methodically gone without pushing the horse to a point where she violently resisted. Together we had built a strong bond of trust. Finally, we were ready to ride as a team, go down the road alone. We would be free.

I rode Nevelee from the driveway out onto the road. We were moving at a slow walk, relaxed, calm, and she responded to my every command. But, rather than being content with a comfortable gait, I wanted to gallop.

We reached a freshly plowed field where the ground was soft and dry. If there were ever a place for me to get thrown off, this site was irresistible. I squeezed my legs together, clicked my tongue and away we went.

As Nevelee ran she began to buck right away, and it wasn't

long before the reins broke and I went flying. The landing was not as soft as expected and my rear-end was stinging. But something hurt me more. I had violated reading my horse's signals. She was not ready to run, I knew that she wasn't … and yet I could not resist indulging my own desire.

My friend continue to buck feverishly, expressing her fear and displeasure in the only way she knew, until she'd worn herself into a hot, droopy heap. Then she allowed me to lead her home.

I talked to her all the way; we were both feeling bad. I was ashamed of my impatience and she was upset because she couldn't buck off the saddle.

Our training sessions continued, and eventually I felt she was ready to be mounted again. Although training a horse was tedious for a sixteen-year-old, I learned more about patience and human behavior than all the psychology classes in dental school.

The key to a relationship is communication. But it has to be on both sides. Nevelee made me aware of intuitions far beyond speech that forced me to increase my other observations. The clues were a look in her eyes, the twitch of an ear, the way she held her head, the pressure on her legs as she stood. People also react instinctively, especially when they're anxious. It's important for us to listen, but also to hone our observation skills so we can pick up signs and feelings that others may be uncomfortable expressing verbally.

Every creature has a unique pace, a speed at which they process concepts, and it's important to attune ourselves to those rhythms, waiting for the proper moment before introducing something new. Often non-verbal indications are the key, though they differ from person to person. By attending to body language and facial expressions we show our respect for those with whom we interact and enhance the communication process. Disrupting someone's natural pace and rhythms can bring disaster.

People are more complex than horses. Then again, we all have the same basic needs, so don't let it throw you.

# A Lesson in Professionalism

*It's a naïve little Burgundy without any breeding,*
*but I think you'll be amused by its presumption.*

– James Thurber

During my junior year of dental school, I was employed by a life insurance company to perform pre-qualifying physicals for potential clients. Many agents were paid on commissions and would attempt to sell insurance to the living dead, so the corporate office needed independent evaluations to protect themselves.

It was a great job that allowed me to hone my physical assessment abilities and improve my chair-side verbal skills. I met interesting people, gained insight into the insurance underwriting system and supplemented my meager income.

The Dean had signed off on my physical assessment skills, so I felt responsible to represent the dental school as professionally as possible.

The other employees engaged in performing physicals were all female nurses, so the stranger businesses and shadier parts of town almost immediately fell under my purview. At first I took these almost daily assignments as a mark of my machismo, but it soon became clear that I was the newbie.

One close, summer night, my last appointment sent me down a narrow street in T-Town. The grass-bare boulevards were lined with parked cars, and men—some of them bare-chested, others wearing T-shirts— milled around in small groups under the street lights or sat on the front stoops of cramps row houses. Windows and doors were propped opened, inviting in the humid air, and also an incongruous, white-smocked dental student carrying a large black case.

My client was a fifty-plus widow named Yvonne. She had short, bleached hair with gray roots parting the center of a Dutchboy cut. Her loosely-tied white halter revealed a generous bosom, and the green short-shorts gave an less flattering look at her thighs.

I asked about her medical history and supplementary income, and then politely proceeded with my physical, measuring her height, weight, blood pressure and pulse before and after exercise. This part of the exam had her hopping on one foot for ten seconds in a jiggle-fest that my eyes could not resist.

Then came the ever-embarrassing request for a urine sample. Provided with a standard pre-packaged cup, Yvonne excused herself and retreated into the privacy of her bathroom.

I sat on the couch waiting to get the hell out of there.

After an unsuccessful try, she came out and apologized. "No problem," I said. "You're my last appointment."

She went into the kitchen, brought out sodas, and we sipped from the cool cans.

"Do you have a special gal?" she asked.

"Oh no, I'm still playing the field."

"That's the way with me, too."

The fan propped in the window was blowing air over my face, cooling me for the first time all day. "I could stay like this for hours."

"Well, maybe you'd be more comfortable it you took off that coat."

"Thanks" I took off the smock, loosened the top button of my shirt and leaned back.

"Better?"

"Yeah, much better."

Her smile revealed a missing left lateral incisor. Suddenly, to my amazement, she moved in next to me, puckering up and piling completely on top of me.

"Whoa!"

I pushed her off, grunted an apology and left without the sample.

Days later, devoid (so to speak) of an explanation, one of the nurses retrieved it.

# A Passion for Life

*There is no end. There is no beginning.*
*There is just the passion of life.*

– Federico Fellini

The young man seemed frozen in a pose. His eyes were closed, but they were sunken deep into his thin, blank skull. His mouth was open, with a fresh, nasty wound to his upper lip. The sutures were gone, but the reddish-purple lip swelled beneath his scraped nose. Half of his shaved head revealed a fresh scar from a life-saving cranial shunt.

The nineteen-year old male had suffered a close head injury with a related facial trauma as a result of a motorcycle accident. The injury to his cranium was significant enough that it left him in a coma. He was breathing on his own, but his long-term prognosis remained unknown.

Although he was still in a coma, his family requested that I check out his dental trauma. I examined his dentition by retracting his placid cheeks and lips, carefully manipulated his mouth so as not to disrupt his lacerated, still-healing lip.

He had fractured several of his front teeth and his upper-left central incisor was avulsed. The facial alveolar bone that supported the tooth was also destroyed.

The young man's story was familiar. Like many recent high school grads, he was wandering aimlessly through life, undecided about his future. He worked part-time pumping gas at a north metro filling station to pay the bills, and drank beer after work with his buds, most of whom were going nowhere fast. Like him.

He had a motorcycle and, of course, rarely wore his helmet. One day he and a friend were running errands on his Honda when they hit loose gravel while attempting to stop at a red light. The bike slipped out from under them. Both were lucky to survive. The driver's upper left mouth was ripped opened by the handle bars and the left side of his head hit the hard concrete road, knocking him unconscious.

The head contusion caused internal swelling inside his cranium, with the amount of brain damage still undetermined.

His rider broke a leg and sustained a large, severe leg burn from the exhaust pipe, but his head (also helmetless) was spared serious head injury.

A MONTH AFTER THE accident, the young man woke up from his coma, and a few days later he was transported to our dental office for a more complete consultation. He arrived in a wheel chair, but he was able to walk slowly on his own.

We reviewed his current medical history, medications, and labs from the chart. He had difficulty processing questions, formulating answers, and even found it difficult to respond to simple requests to open or close his mouth. His conversation was labored, the thought patterns disjointed—clearly his synapses were not all firing yet.

After radiographs and impressions, I was able to offer several options for his future dental treatment. Because he was clearly incapable of making long-term decisions, I consulted with his parents, who decided to start with a bone-tissue graft.

During a follow-up appointment, he told me that while he was in a coma, he had a long conversation with his older sister, Anita. They spent days discussing their family and his life. After a month, when he woke up, his sister never showed up at the hospital and when he asked for her, his parents changed the subject. He eventually was informed that Anita had passed away two years earlier. The doctors had waited until he was strong enough to re-grieve her death, hoping the trauma would not delay his recovery.

This piece of sad news, if anything, made these conversations more precious than ever. The young man would mentally rehash them repeatedly, pondering the advice that his sister had given him. Anita had told him how to live the rest of his life. She asked him who he admired most. She told him to find someone who seemed to be living life the 'right way.' Was there a family member or someone who was living a dream life? When he found that person, he should ask for help, get advice and go for it, live the life of his dreams without regrets.

"My conversations with Anita were real," he insisted.

By the time he came in for the bridge preparation, he was almost completely recovered, with fresh hair covering his skeletal scars. His attitude was upbeat and he had chosen to emulate a family friend, a self-employed printer with a nice family who was rich in more ways than money.

Six months later his dental rehabilitation was complete. The time had passed quickly, and dental work aside, he was now soaring, working nights, going to trade school during the day, learning all he could about the printing industry. His mentor had given him a start on a new career path and instilled dreams of success.

On the relationship side, although he had not yet found the love of his life, he was attempting to treat women with the same respect he'd developed for his sister Anita.

Learning patience and the rewards of hard work, he was finally living his life with a new passion.

# Haitian Dentist

*Good judgment comes from experience,*
*and experience comes from bad judgment.*

– Rita Mae Brown

On steamy autumn day in San Francisco, during a break at an American Dental Association (ADA) meeting I was attending, I cut through the back door of my hotel and walked across the alley to a sports bar. When I sat down on the only available stool at the bar the woman next to me burst out laughing.

"You don't know what you just did," she sputtered as she tried to catch her breath.

"What did I do?"

"You see that line of people?" she gestured vague toward the front door, which stood opposite to the one I'd ducked in through. "They've all been waiting patiently in line, and you just walked in and sat down."

I lowered my head in mock embarrassment. "Well, I guess I'm with you today."

She was a petite Hispanic in her mid-thirties with gold-rimmed glasses and an ADA name badge that identified her as Haitian. I know little about Haiti, and she was equally ill-acquainted with Minnesota, so we explored our mutual ignorance of one another's geography, cultures, and life-styles over a cold beer. She was curious about life in a cold climate I attempted to get a flavor of her world by showering her with questions. A picture soon emerged of a woman who led a privileged life. Her wealth derived from a family-owned rum distillery that had recently lost profitability. With an increase in rum popularity in the Caribbean, her family was trying to re-invest.

Her work was not much different from mine. She was in a solo practice in a metropolitan area and worked thirty-four hours a week. She was here to improve her dental education, learn what was new in dentistry and to escape her island for a little while. A long string of murders had been committed in her country; the servants of the wealthy were killing their bosses and absconding with processions. The current government was unstable and the police were riddled with corruption. She had several domestic servants herself, and was afraid to go back home after the convention. Yet the poverty was so great that people were regularly employed to do all kinds of menial domestic work. She had refrained from buying a washing machine or clothes dryer, because it would have put people out of work.

Curious to learn more about such seemingly kind, if paternalistic, relations, I asked: "What type dental care do you do for the poor?"

"I don't do any dentistry unless I get paid."

I was stunned; how calloused she seemed to her own people.

"You don't understand. Women are second-class citizens in Haiti. As a professional woman, it is my passion to advocate for women's rights. That seems a lot more important to me than trying to solve every dental problem under the sun gratis."

My values, in my world, did not make sense in hers.

Altruism is personal.

# Respected in Life and Death

*The human face is an empty power, a field of death ...*
*after countless thousands of years that the human face*
*has spoken and breathed, one still has the impression*
*that it hasn't even begun to say what it is*
*and what it knows.*

– Antonin Artaud (1896-1948)

Cadaver is a strange noun. The word does not convey the reality of a lifeless human body. It gentrifies the leathery, formaldehyde-soaked corpse succumbing to our intimate dissection.

The Gross Human Anatomy course offers a comprehensive understanding of all physical aspects of the human body with a combination of classroom didactics and laboratory dissections. An entire year is devoted to the subject, and memorization of all the body pieces and parts is required.

I approached the class and cadavers with curiosity and trepidation. My own human form made it more relevant than most of my dental courses. But I had some anxiety about my ability to cut up a body, and wondered how the act might affect me.

Our first lecture began with a lesson on respect for the dead. Some altruistic person had donated the use of their body to help others gain valuable knowledge. Respect for these human remains must never be violated, with reverence for the solemn result we all reach.

Our cadavers were wrapped in green cloths to retain the moisture with formaldehyde, and the smell was more revolting than the sight. The first exposure we saw was of several bare backs and some de-skinned musculature. But the view was not distressing, and we were relieved that none of us threw up or passed out.

With the exception of the head and neck, we were gradually introduced to all body parts. Soon we became desensitized to the odor, spending hours manipulating and dissecting the dead. Even as our classmates were humped over a smelly, exposed cadaver, we sometimes paused for a snack. No body parts were allowed outside the lab, and any student tempting to pilfer them would be expelled immediately.

As it turned out, I loved learning about my body through the looking glass the cadavers offered. The black lungs of a smoker and the ravages of cancer were opened and on display for all of us to see. Here was physical evidence of the consequences that accompany the choices we make in life.

It reminded me of what the Catholic nuns used to drum into our heads -- our bodies are God's temples and we need to treat them as such.

However, disease is not a judgment, and the anatomical and genetic variations are totally out of our control. During the class death was addressed only briefly, as a rare outcome of poor judgment or a failure to activate emergency services during a heart attack. This was my introduction to clinical death and daily living with human mortality.

The heads of our cadavers were unveiled during the second half of the year. Each face was a unique structure with its own distinctive shape, a summation of individual features, nose size, projection, lip fullness, width, eye shapes, hair color, length, hairline, forehead, cheekbones, chins short and long, all singularly spaced to create the silhouette of their humanity. Curiously, the teeth did not seem to matter anymore.

Most troubling to me was that suddenly each individual's face took on the reality of a human life. For months these cadavers had given us hands-on experience with the working organs of what we knew were dead people; but the face revealed a personality and an identity that I was no longer able to deny. The lady with multiple surgeries altering her organ anatomy looked like my seventh-grade teacher. The body known for his well-defined muscle structure was revealed to be an innocent-faced young man.

For weeks I was preoccupied about why these people had shared their deceased bodies with science. Should I share my organs, eyes, body parts and pieces that might further the quality of life for others? Our bodies only decay after our death, so why not help mankind with knowledge that may positively affect the future?

I finally came to grips with the great gift these people were sharing with our class. In their death, they gave the gift of knowledge that allows us to give better treatment for hundreds of our patients, now and in the future.

The temples of these anonymous lives were our teachers, and their souls are left in God's good hands.

## "Just Like in the National Geographic"

*Success is getting what you want.*
*Happiness is wanting what you get.*

– Dale Carnegie

I was standing in the nurse's station at The Sister Kinney Institute mentally digesting the hospital chart of my new "dental consult" patient, Fred, when the nurse approached and said, "Remember when you were a kid and *National Geographic* magazine had pictures of Africans doing weird things to their lips? Well, this patient's lip is much worse."

Her comments only sparked my curiosity. The chart revealed that Fred had suffered a high spinal cord injury as result of a motor vehicle accident and was currently in a semi-comatose state. He was not responsive to verbal commands. He was able to breathe on his own without the assistance of a ventilator, but had permanently lost all feeling from the neck down.

As I walked down the hall with the information from the chart and the warning from the nurse swirling in my head, I braced myself for the unexpected. Carrying my black dental bag with limited supplies I walked into the room and immediately understood what the nurse had meant by her warning. Lying in a large hospital bed was an eighteen-year-old adolescent who looked much younger than his age and appeared to be sleeping. As I walked closer to the bed I focused on his lips; shockingly, both upper and lower lips appeared to be swollen hunks of chewed up hamburger. They were raw from self-mutilation. The whole circumference of his mouth was bloody and swollen.

It appeared that in his unconscious state he was uncontrollably masticating his own lips.

During a visual oral exam I ascertained that other than his lips, Fred's dentition and the rest of his oral cavity was normal and in good repair. They had no idea how long it would take for him to recover from his unconscious state, but they were optimistic that the coma would only be temporary. The physician, and more importantly the family, wondered if there was anything I could do to prevent him from continually damaging his lip. This is not something that I had previous experience with. Basically, it required creative problem-solving skills to devise something that would help the patient without raising the risk of added harm.

In short, I needed to construct some type of oral appliance that would prevent Fred from biting his lips. This would require getting dental impressions of his upper and lower teeth. We had no idea if the patient's gag reflex was still intact, however, and the challenge would be to keep the impression material away from his throat. The risk was that some loose matter would end up in his lungs. I was also concerned that he might unintentionally dislodge whatever appliance I would create while moving his lips.

I had worked with patients in the past who had suffered either spinal cord injuries or closed head injuries. Among such patients oral self-mutilation is a common sight. There is nothing in the professional literature, as far as I know, to account for the behavior, but I have my own theory regarding such "neuralgenic bruxism and "self-stimuli trauma."

Imagine you're in a coma or semi-coma and have lost all feeling from the neck down. Your only sensations come from in and around your head. As you fight the symptoms of the coma and the huge physical trauma your body has endured, suddenly, in your semi-comatose state, you discover you can stimulate yourself by biting your lip. It's almost like touching yourself in the morning to realize you're here and awake. Such self-stimulation may help your brain work its way back to a conscious state. The question arises: Will an appliance designed to prevent a patient from hurting himself delay his recovery? We don't really know. At this point, our objective is to satisfy the request of the family to prevent the patient from hurting himself.

Once the physician and the patient's family had accepted my plan, I fabricated two soft mouth guards that when placed over Fred's teeth would displace the lips outward enough that he wouldn't be able to bite them. I attached a string or tether to both guards and attached them to his clothes with a safety pin; if they happened to get dislodged we'd be able to retrieve them. I showed the nurse how to insert the guard and told them to call me should problems arise.

A couple days had gone by and no one had called, so I assumed things were coming along as we hoped. I decided to stop by and see after three days and was surprised by the results. There is an old adage that states, "Be careful what you wish for." I was hoping that the patient's lips had healed and that he had woken up from his coma. Not only had his lips heal, but because they'd been so raw and abraded, the corners of his mouth had healed together, leaving the opening smaller—too small to do much further work on the inside of his mouth.

Fred was still in a semi-comatose state, but there were signs that he was improving. The family was thrilled with the results, as was I, though I felt it necessary to warn them at some point in the future, surgery might be required to re-open the corners of their son's mouth.

I can gladly report that Fred did completely recover from the coma and proceeded to undergo intensive rehab in order to cope with his permanent complete quadriplegia. He was fitted for a large motorized wheelchair controlled by a sip-and-puff device attached to a straw-like tube. Normally, with the straw placed between his lips, a patient, through a combination of sips and puffs, can navigate the hallways of life. Unfortunately Fred had traumatized his lips to such a degree that he no longer had any sensation in his lips and could not create the seal required to sip or puff. His trauma to his lips had left him immobile.

I was called back in to see what I could do about the problem of Fred's lips. I returned to the hospital, observed the patient in his shiny new black motorized wheelchair, and returned to my office with one of the sip-and-puff straws. I started to experiment with the dental plastics and acrylics that we use for different things in dentistry, and found a thermal plastic material that would bond to the straw. This material could be modified to any shape or size by applying heat. I added a flange to the end of the straw and brought it back to the hospital, along with a torch and some lab equipment, in case I needed to further customize the straw to Fred's mouth.

Before long Fred was driving his chair with ease. I never anticipated that I, as a dentist, would be given the opportunity to help with the mobility of a quadriplegic. The patient, the family and the tech were all heartily grateful for my ingenuity, but I had more fun than I can describe. I know that dentistry helps maintain a quality of life, but contributing to Fred's road to recovery has improved his quality of life beyond any dental restoration I've done.

Eventually sensation did return to Fred's lips, and my customizes straw was no longer needed. I was happy to learn that Fred recently earned a college degree. People can accomplish amazing things when they put their mind to work. Fred mastered the lesson of living to live, and I was honored to play a small part in that personal success.

# The Tuba Player

*The policy of being too cautious*
*is the greatest risk of all.*

– Jawaharial Nehru

One spectacular fall afternoon a young emergency patient with traumatic injury was unexpectedly added to my schedule. When he arrived, accompanied by his mother, we seated him immediately in an operatory. His lip was swollen and red, though there was no sign of a laceration. He had fractured both front teeth at about forty-five degrees from the normal bite line. The middle corners were gone and the pulps of both teeth were hanging out.

"So, tell me what happened." The boy hung down his head. His mother attempted to answer but then began to sob, "I wouldn't let him play football, I refused basketball, no way on earth would I allow him to take up hockey. Finally I said no to soccer. But I let him play in the school band and he ran into a wall with a tuba in his mouth."

We want to shield our children from pain and suffering, but at some point they need to fall down and learn to get up on their own. Experience is far better than over-protection, and as this young man's experience shows, there's really no way to know from what direction injury may arrive. The road map is different for each individual, but the destination is the same: to raise a productive adult who's able to assay risks and take a few of them. It takes maturity to be selfless when we raise our children.

# Beyond Appearances

## An Angel Unawares

*Forget not to show love unto strangers: for thereby some have entertained angels unawares.*

– Hebrews 13:2

I'd been asked to evaluate the mouth pain of an adolescent female in the lock-up at St. Mary's Hospital. She was deemed a high risk for running away so the staff requested that I see her on site. The medical chart of this thirteen-year-old girl described an underworld life so horrible it was beyond belief, and when I read it I was stunned.

She was born to high school drop-outs who spent most of their life on the streets of Minneapolis. To support their daily dependency on drugs, they forced their daughter to join her mother in prostitution. Her hard life had left her with physical scars, needle tracks, illnesses and mental delay. She had experienced de-tox and was screened for every known sexually-transmitted disease under the sun.

I walked in expecting a hard-nosed kid with the exaggerated make-up of a hooker, a tough broad who could chew the heads off of nails.

Instead, a shy, petite young lady was sitting on the examination table. She had brown eyes and light, slightly-freckled skin. Her hair was straight and clean. Her small arms showed signs of needle marks with random scratches. She had the appearance of a nine-year-old, and her innocence penetrated deep into my soul. I thought of her as Angel.

I introduced myself and asked about her dental problems. She indicated several loose, painful teeth in the back of her mouth which my gloved fingers were able to wiggle. Not only was her physical development delayed, she still had her baby teeth. Angel was just a baby.

There were no signs of cavities, but she needed a complete set of radiographs to determine all of her dental needs, and we escorted her to our office to take them. There were also some issues of spacing between her teeth that required an orthodontic evaluation, so she was scheduled the next morning at the hospital clinic.

When I went to the hospital clinic the next day, the door was wide open, Angel was reclined in the chair and the orthodontist was inspecting her mouth with his bare hands swimming in her saliva.

I tapped him on the shoulder, motioned him aside and whispered, "Did you read her chart?" He shook his head. "Wash your hands and read the chart."

He leafed through the pages, his face slowly turning red. His breath came faster and periodically he sighed. Finally he washed his hands several times, put on protective gloves and resumed his examination.

Afterward, we talked about Angel's dental needs, discussed extractions and future space concerns. Basically, the plan was to remove her primary teeth and allow her permanent teeth to erupt normally.

Angel's parents were both incarcerated at the time, so the nurse's station contacted her guardian grandmother, who gave her consent. With her guardian's permission, we would remove her baby teeth at our office that afternoon.

It's routine for locked-up patients to be dressed in attire that would make it difficult for them to run away. That afternoon Angel was brought to our office wearing pajamas and slippers. She was not fearful, but cooperative and eager to get rid of those aggravating teeth.

Everything went well. Gauze packs were placed over the fresh extraction sites, with a few extra given to her until the bleeding stopped. A pamphlet on the procedure was reviewed, instructions written in her chart. She was excused and a staff member brought her back to the lock-up. I never saw her or heard from her again.

But this saintly child continues to reverberate in my daily life. I imagined that Angel and other abused children would be placed in foster care in our neighborhoods or in our communities. Therefore, I needed to be a responsible parent and I needed to enthusiastically educate, council and support my children on all the taboo subjects of our world; sex, drugs, abuse, mental illness, and other issues that I would previously have tried to shield them from.

My desire was to remain naïve, imagining I could identify and avoid certain zones of experience, but after treating Angel, I can never look at anybody the same way again. My personal prejudices, sociological generalizations, and egotistical holier-than-thou attitudes were blown out of the water forever by that single encounter. We fool ourselves into thinking we can characterize people by their appearance. Is it our tendency to prejudge others just to satisfy our own inability to deal with all the unknowns?

When choosing dentistry as a career, I never gave much thought to the long-term impact individual patients might have in my life. On what new road will my next patient take me?

What happened to Angel? Did she make it?

# The Star of David

*Question with boldness even the existence of a God;*
*because, if there be one, he must more approve of*
*the homage of reason, than that of blind-folded fear.*

– Thomas Jefferson

His shiny black boots were laced up to his knees. Dressed in black, sporting Nazi swastikas on two arm bands, hair slicked back, Larry Trapp was a self-professed Nazi who wore the uniform daily and without apology. He boldly leaned on the wall waiting for his appointment at the University of Nebraska Dental School.

The "Nazi guy" visited so often, I assumed he had a lot of dental needs. Severe diabetes would later account for his frequent appearances. With his inability to fight off infections, he was prone to severe gum disease.

Trapp's racist antics and hate crimes were often described in the Lincoln press. He was anti-Semitic, anti-Catholic, and rumored to be Grand Dragon in the Ku Klux Klan. He preached bigotry on his own cable access channel and had acquired a daunting criminal rap sheet as a result of his hateful behavior.

Years later, after I had established a practice in Minneapolis, I was driving to work one morning when I heard on the radio that one of the city's numerous theatre groups, In the Heart of the Beast Puppet and Mask Theater, was going to put on a play about Larry Trapp. The title, "Befriended by the Enemy," clued me in to the fact that there would be a surprising twist to the story. I attended one evening, and found myself enthralled by a remarkable story of conversion and faith.

In 1991, Trapp had harassed a Jewish cantor, Michael Weisser, and his wife, Julie, bombarding them with obscene phone calls at their home in Lincoln. One day, in response to yet another call, the cantor told Trapp, who had had a foot amputated from diabetes, that if he needed help with getting groceries, Weisser would stop by his house, get a list, and go to the store. Trapp agreed. Before he left on the unusual errand, Michael told his wife that if he didn't return home within a reasonable span of time, to call the police.

When Weisser arrived at Trapp's apartment, he was surprised to see how small it was. Firearms were spread throughout the room and Nazi flags were hanging on the walls. But Trapp himself was civil enough, and before long the cantor and his wife began routinely bringing groceries to Trapp, talking with him, and helping him out in other ways. Eventually their kindness got through to the man. Trapp begged for their forgiveness, and even went so far as to convert to Judaism. In 1992, he spent the last two months of his life at home with the Weissers and their two small children.

I shared this story with college classmates at our twenty-fifth reunion at the University of Nebraska. Many of them remembered him well. One classmate sheepishly admitted, "You know, I was working on the Nazi Guy and he needed a gold crown on his tooth. Right before cementing it, I carved the Star of David inside."

May wonders never cease.

## Betty Jean

*The idea of death, the fear of it, haunts the human animal like nothing else; it is a mainspring of human activity—designed largely to avoid the fatality of death, to overcome it by denying in some way that it is the final destiny of man.*

– Ernest Becker

Betty Jean was a bright woman who played the role of caregiver her whole life. Professionally, she was a nurse. She was the mother of two. Married for many years, she and her husband had recently separated. The kids were grown and gone, but her mother came to live with Betty Jean for several years. When she died, Billy Jean had no one left to care for. Still, she enjoyed gardening and cooking.

I found her to be a pleasant dental patient, though she was reluctant to improve her dentition even slightly beyond what her dental insurance would cover. A victim of insurance maximums and her insurer's definition of "usual and customary" treatment, she often settled for less-than-ideal treatment.

When she was diagnosed with pancreatic cancer she knew her prognosis was not good.

Soon thereafter she appeared in my dental chair with a lower incisor that had broken off. She told me about the cancer and said, "Just fix the tooth so I can look good in the casket." It really needed a buildup and crown. But during her years as a nurse Betty Jean had seen many patients with pancreatic cancer die quite suddenly, and wanted only a quick, inexpensive repair for her tooth. I fixed the tooth with a large resin that I knew would only be a temporary patch. When it was time for her to leave, she reached out and grabbed my knee, looked into my eyes, and told me goodbye. She did not expect to see me again, and reaching into my heart, she wanted me to know that *this was it*. As she slowly walked down the hall I was struck with deep sorrow, and simultaneous felt a wave of gratitude for having had her as a patient. The intensity of the emotion made me feel uncomfortable that I had to treat the next patient on the schedule.

A MONTH LATER, Betty Jean's former husband was in the office. He told me she was in the hospital, was very ill, and he didn't know if she was going to make it. I was in the habit of reading the obituaries routinely, but as the months went by, Betty Jean's name failed to appear.

Then one day I saw her name on my schedule for a crown. She arrived looking great. "They kicked me out of hospice care," she announced with a sparkle in her eye.

In our next conversation, Betty Jean shared what she had learned since her cancer diagnosis. She had been hospitalized, not because of the cancer, but for a spastic colon she'd developed due to the stress of the cancer diagnosis. Released from the hospital, she was placed in hospice care, where her health improved so much that she "flunked out. " She then scheduled an appointment with a new oncologist, who told her she had been misdiagnosed.

She had told everybody she was going to die, and given away most of her belongings. Now she was eager to reclaim them. She also had to reclaim her life. After a lifetime of caretaking and a near-surrender of her own life, Betty Jean is no longer interested in "getting by." She got the crown. Next on her agenda was getting her cataracts fixed. "It never occurred to me," she marveled, "that quality of life is all we have while we're here on earth."

Improving the quality of life is what I'm about as a dentist. I succeed when I help make life easier for someone. Another hospice patient reinforced my determination when he asked me to reline an ill-fitting denture. I knew I could improve his life, regardless of how long it lasted, by helping him eat and speak better. The man lived two weeks with his relined denture. The out pouring of his family's gratitude will stay with me for the rest of my life— however long or short it is.

All of us find that our lives have more meaning when others value our existence and our talents. Sometimes a simple "thank you" is all the fulfillment we need.

# The Bite

*Patience is the companion of wisdom.*

– Saint Augustine

Just when you think you've seen it all, Thelma is in your chair. She's a resident from a nursing home who has been coming for years. On this occasion, it was a follow-up appointment to restore a couple of cavities. When she arrived, we were expecting a simple, unremarkable visit.

As usual, Thelma was transported to our office by a company called Metro-Mobility. The driver had brought along a copy of her nursing home chart, which I reviewed before my assistant seated her. Her main diagnosis was "Senile Dementia." Everything else was typical for an eighty-year-old nursing home patient. I saw nothing in the chart that would complicate our treatment that day, so I recommended that she be seated in one of our rooms for her restorative care.

As I followed her into the room, I did a brief physical assessment of the patient. Thelma's hair was dark-orange, similar to a clown's wig. I assumed they had attempted to dye it red but missed the mark. She wore an old house dress with tiny blue flowers on it. Her nylons were rolled up at the knees and one of them had a pack of cigarettes stuck in the top . She was wearing black, thick shoes that were scuffed and unpolished. Her make-up appeared to have been self-applied without the aid of a mirror. The best that could be said of the deep red lipstick was that it was *close* to her lips. She also had big circles of red rouge on her cheeks, as if she were set for a night on the town. By the look of it, her hands and eyes just didn't work as well as they used to.

If I were in a nursing home, I'm sure I'd consider it a blessing to get dressed up from time to time and leave the premises. On such occasions, the nursing home staff will make a special effort to make the patient look good, because the outside world often forms its opinions of the care inside the facility based on the hygiene of the patients when they leave. They will be bathed, dressed in their Sunday Best, and perhaps get their hair done. It might be cheaper for the home to bring professionals in to provide dental and medical care, but arranging for an occasional outing can do the patient a world of good in itself.

Thelma was a pleasant lady; she responded civilly to my greetings, and we carried on a brief and unremarkable conversation before I explained that she was here to get a couple of teeth fixed, and the two cavities would require some local anesthetic. This news didn't seem to trouble her. Everything was fine. We placed a topical anesthetic on the site to numb the place where the injection would be given, so it wouldn't hurt. The injection went well and we waited a short time for it to take affect. I told her that if she needed a break or if she was feeling pain during thew drilling, to raise her left hand and we would stop.

As we began to work in her mouth she immediately bit down on my finger. She was biting hard enough so that I couldn't remove my finger, but not hard enough to cause much pain. As I tugged to remove my finger, I noticed the delight in her eyes. Her face was filled with joy and her expression showed how happy she was with her current accomplishment.

I tugged again to no avail and said, "Open please." With a smile, she released my hand and joyfully declared, "If you hurt me, then I'll hurt you!"

I was tempted to cross that diagnosis of "Senile Dementia" off her chart that day. She showed me who was in control and I've been laughing ever since.

# The Dental Tango

*Life is a shipwreck but we must not*
*forget to sing in the life boats.*

– Voltaire

The dance between the dentist and the patient is unpredictable. Each person's style requires a unique choreography. Some take the Two-Step, others require the Waltz, but with Tanya it was definitely the Tango.

She lay reclined in a motorized wheelchair: bellowing cheeks, bright eyes, curly, muddy-red-blond hair, huge lips, exaggerated make-up, no neck, hands that appeared to be plastic and a small ovoid body wrapped in a dress. A mouth stick was attached to the wheelchair near her chin as she gasped rhythmically for air.

Polio had affected Tanya's spinal column at a level of C-3 at a young age in the 1950s. Her lungs were not involved, but the intercostal muscles of her chest, abdomen and diaphragm were paralyzed.

Most people in this condition are confined to an iron lung, but Tanya was an exception. She skilled herself in getting people to do what she couldn't. And for routine dental care without hospitalization, she taught me to perform the "Dental Tango."

The procedure we developed involved brief invasive interruptions to work on Tanya's teeth in the midst of her agonized breathing. She would gulp, gulp, gulp, then I would drill for five seconds and get out. Gulp, gulp, gulp. Drill five seconds. Get out. The routine became second nature. Sometimes she would speak between gulps; the pattern continued for the whole time she was in the chair. I was particularly proud of myself the day we restored a maxillary second molar using this painstakingly slow approach. On prior visits I feared that Tanya become overly dependant on our office for her care, ironically I now realized that Tanya had just trained me well.

Sometimes I'd go to her high-rise condo in downtown St. Paul to conduct a limited visual exam and clean her teeth with a portable hand piece. She was on state assistance, which made the high-tech quality of her home all the more surprising. For example, her iron lung had a life-sustaining back-up generator—not the easiest item to locate in the housing market.

Tanya also required a personal attendant to feed, bath, move her and perform all daily activities, and it was apparent their special relationship was built on intimate trust.

Tanya was a dictator. She learned early that if she did not demand the care she needed, she would not survive. She was driven to manipulate, insist, coerce and just plain bully. She did not exclude herself.

Tanya's body was forced into a new form. Her cheeks were huge because she bellowed them to swallow the maximum amount of air. Her neck was wide, allowing an expanded airway from the base of her skull to her shoulders. The shape of her head had been altered by the air-tight seals on the face masks and elastics she wore. Her mouth had developed a big anterior open bite from the wooden mouth stick she used to operate her computer.

The lack of a working diaphragm and chest muscles affected her ability to clear her lungs. The secretions that accumulate there can act as glue, preventing the lungs from inflating properly and causing them to collapse (atelectasia), resulting in upper respiratory infections and pneumonia. Several doctors told her that she would not survive this condition, but she outlived many of them.

She miraculously learned to control her epiglottis mentally, thus obviating the need for a ventilator hook-up that would have limited her mobility. Fewer than twenty people in the world have learned the art of "pharyngeal breathing."

Tanya was personally affected by the meddling of the legislature over benefits and program cuts. She lobbied successfully on behalf of the disabled, and she was elected 'Miss Wheelchair Minnesota.'

Tanya was our dental patient for more than fifteen years and she never had a bad day. She was a fighter who showed us that attitude can do it all. If we can't control what knocks us down, we can choose how we react to it.

For Tanya, it was the dance.

# Hope

*I live on hope and that I think do*
*all who come into this world.*

– Robert Bridges

The young African man's front tooth was hanging down about a quarter of an inch from the rest of his teeth, but he appeared not to be suffering from any acute pain. His only complaint was that he had difficulty chewing his food with this loose tooth hanging down in the way.

We had been acting as a dental consultant for the Center for Victims of Torture, a Minneapolis-based non-profit, which provided a variety of services for refugees from war-torn countries from all over the globe. Coincidentally, it was founded by the Governor of Minnesota, Rudy Perpich, who had been a dentist before entering public life.

Due to limited resources, we were able to treat only the worst cases of dental pain and dental emergencies until the patients qualified for Medicaid or some other type of insurance.

This small young black man was from a French-speaking part of Africa. He spoke very little English, so he was escorted to our office by an interpreter provided by the Center. She was a very beautiful, petite white woman who was quite soft spoken. It was apparent very quickly that these two were very compatible and had already established a good working relationship.

We started our normal routine by taking a medical history and a radiograph of the area of complaint. But that day the medical history was anything but routine. A simple review of the man's bodily systems revealed a history of heinous torture. The litany of abuses was all the more powerful, coming from the mouth of this petite goddess-figure of a woman. Like many others who don't actually *know* the language, I associate the sound of French, which is soft to the ears, with traditional romance, and the shock of having his graceful conversation translated into brutal English made the reality of his torture even harsher.

I maintained eye-contact with the man as I asked him questions in English. As I spoke the young lady's soft voice interpreted quickly in an unobtrusive manner. He also maintained eye contact with me as she spoke, hoping to get visual confirmation of understanding. The dance of words proceeded as follows; "Are you in good health?" Shaking his head "No, I have problems, but the Center and their doctors are trying to fix them." I proceeded read a list of bodily systems and diseases, and soon the flood gates opened and he freely shared and his past physical insults.

He spoke in the rhythmic French song-like conversation looking directly into my eyes and not blinking as he spewed out his story. He acknowledged a chronic rectal bleed as a result of being sodomized with a broom handle. He shared that he had been stuffing rags in his rectum periodically to stop the bleeding, along with other intimate details of a litany of tortuous acts—shared them with me, a complete stranger called upon to address his dental needs.

As this beautiful woman translates his story, my acquired poker face attempts to hide my disgust with the indecencies he has borne. Empathetically I listen as his continues to review his internal and external wounds. Spleen was traumatized. Stomach was stabbed with a knife. He was electrocuted and sustained multiple beatings. Multiple scars on his exposed skin, randomly distributed, confirm his heart-felt tale.

The front tooth was struck during one of the many beatings he suffered, and was avulsed from its normal socket. The radiograph revealed that there was no longer any bone support left. I regretfully informed him that there was no way to keep the tooth. It would have to be extracted.

He will have many options for replacement to choose from, including fixed and removable bridges made of several different materials. After I explain the situation at some length, he finally seems to accept that the tooth needs to be removed and can be replaced, for the time being, with a temporary removable partial.

In the process of preparing for the construction of a temporary upper partial that would replace the terminal tooth, we gave him a mirror and held up tooth shade tabs next to his existing teeth for him to choose from. When I held the tab that in my eyes was a perfect match to his teeth, he suddenly launched into a long interrogative dissertation. The interpreter had difficulty translating his words; I patiently waited for his new comments. "He wants to know if he can have his teeth bleached," the interpreter finally shared.

My first reaction was one of fleeting disgust, directed not at the patient, but at my own affluent culture, which placed such a narcissistic concentration on such things as the esthetic superiority of "white teeth." Here was a man who had been through a hell unimaginably to most of us. After spending only a few weeks in America, he had already been corrupted by the trivial values that dominate our media.

But almost on my next breath that feeling of disgust was replaced by a sense of hope. Weighed down by a host of infirmities inflicted upon him by his fellow man, this survivor retained the desire to improve himself in this land of endless opportunities. In has been an honor for me to be a small part of the rehabilitation process, and to see more than a few refugees regaining their sense of hope and opportunity with the help of The Center for Victims of Torture. That institution is something our culture can take pride in.

# A Beautiful Woman

*Beauty without grace is the hook without the bait.*

– Ralph Waldo Emerson

Anne was always well kept. She was the only daughter of a rural Iowa county sheriff, attractive and pleasing to the eye, yet I never considered her a beautiful woman.

It had been a few years since I'd seen Anne in my dental office, so when I saw her name on my schedule it summoned up her stunning physical memory.

She was a tall, sleek, woman who would never be seen without her perfectly applied make-up. Her sandy hair was highlighted with blond streaks and flawlessly puffed up on top of her head, revealing her long, graceful neck. When she smiled, her straight, white teeth were the centerpiece of an elegantly tanned, symmetrical face. She held her chin high with pride. Her upright posture and square shoulders transmitted self-confidence.

I looked forward to her visit and anticipated exchanging pleasantries with her.

To my surprise, when I entered the room for her appointment a much older lady was slouched in the dental chair. Her clothes were wrinkled and limply draped over her thin frame. A cheap sandy gray wig drooped over the side of her gaunt face like an old mop. As I caught a glimpse of her face, I finally realized it was Anne from her distinctive gold-rimmed glasses. Illness had accelerated the aging process; she was not the same fearless mountain of strength that I once knew.

Her eyelashes and eyebrows were missing and not one ounce of makeup was spent masking her deeply wrinkled, leather-like face.

'Our eyes finally met, and her deep blue eyes pierced mine. I felt as if I were melting away with stunned sympathy.

Her appearance released a haunting memory of my father's old Chris Craft cabin cruiser after I had left home for college. It was left stranded and dry-docked for a few years in the stark confines of our desolate backyard. During that period without its seasonal maintenance it was hammered defenselessly by the elements. The silhouette of its former grandeur didn't change but the exterior had become a caved-in, decaying, unsightly wreck. The ravages of time and weather had stripped the vessel of its glistening beauty and its majesty, turning it into a heap of gray, rotting planking that would never again be seaworthy.

Putting on my poker face, I washed my hands and said, "Welcome back, stranger. It has been a while. How's the family?"

Anne straightened up in the chair, lifted up her chin and pulled her shoulders back. She now appeared as if she were glowing. Floating like a heavenly angelic spirit, her voice, her eyes, and her body emanated with grace and love.

She proudly relayed, "Well, my husband, Dan, is in the nursing home recovering from cancer surgery and we'll get him back home soon. I am so glad. I miss him dearly. Now I'm fighting my own bout with cancer. I am so lucky. My grandson is divine. I have my family and people like you in my life." She flashed me a small, subtle grin. I melted.

I felt a warm blanket of love surround me and also an aura of peace. The cobwebs that had gathering in the corners of my brain were swept aside by her spirit, and I was suddenly struck by the reality of all the gifts that bless my life—gifts that I too often took for granted.

She turned to me and grabbed my heart again with those blazing blue eyes.

"I was so excited when I got notice that you bought this practice. It's right down the street from me with free parking. You are the only dentist in the world I could ever see."

I was humbled by the loyalty of a lost angel. There were no words to describe how beautiful she had become.

# The Paranoid Schizophrenic

*People only see what they are prepared to see.*

– Ralph Waldo Emerson

Ted's massive frame crashed through my office door at 6:30 AM, a full thirty minutes early. The door banged violently against the wall, sending a thunderous boom echoing up and down the halls. If I had not met him previously, Ted's rude and dramatic appearance would have terrified me. As it was, I knew he was harmless from past experiences, so I greeted him courteously, as always. A frazzled mop of brownish-gray shoulder-length hair covered his homely face. His glasses were partially fogged over and mended at one corner of the frame with white adhesive tape. He wore a filthy gray parka with fake fur lining the hood, and carried, strapped to his back, an old black backpack that gave him the appearance of the Hunchback of Notre Dame.

The unbuckled buckles of his old rubber galoshes clanked as he strode into the reception room. The zipper on his parka was pulled halfway down to reveal a dingy white T-shirt under a wool plaid Macinaw. After hanging up his coat on an otherwise empty coat rack, Ted commenced to tell us about the wicked crow that had followed him all the way from his apartment to our office. He expressed the hope that the crow would not be not outside waiting for him when he left. He sat briefly but was unable to sit still, and after fidgeting briefly in the chair he got up and left the office. Minutes later he returned to the room and whined in a deep monotone voice, "The antibiotics gave me diarrhea you know." That was more information than I wanted to know, considering how unwashed he looked.

Ted was scheduled for a routine periodontal maintenance appointment with the hygienist and an oral exam with me. After forty-five minutes I was summoned to the hygienists operatory. As I walked in the room the odor hit me like a wall—a combination of stale smoke and putridly intense body odor that made my eyes water. I would have welcomed freshly cut onions.

I put on my facial mask (hoping against hope that it would muffle the odor) and my high powered magnification examination glasses, and then bellied up to the chair. The huge acne pores on Ted's reddened, greasy face grew more forbidding still under magnification. His ears and nose sprouted bunches of hair and I spotted a few remnants of his runny eggs caked to his wispy beard. When he opened his mouth, I took a look at his swollen, blood-lined gums and ragged margins, trying my best not to inhale the nauseating stench any more deeply than I had to. After detecting a couple of troubled or rotting lesions, I politely excused myself to address the needs of others patients. Ted received an appointment to return the following week.

The minute he left the office my hygienist informed me that Ted's cat had died and he was talking about suicide. I phoned his psychiatrist with the news. He thanked me for the information and reassured me that he would handle it. Meanwhile, I began to wonder why someone who was contemplating suicide would worry about getting their teeth cleaned?

David returned a week later for the scheduled follow up. "How are you doing?" I greeted him.

He replied in his low monotone voice, "I probably shouldn't tell after what happened last week."

Confused by his response, I inquired "Why? What happened last week?"

"After I left your office last week I went home and the police kicked down my apartment door and hauled me down to Hennepin County Medical Center for a Psych evaluation. So I probably shouldn't say anymore."

I knew he had something more to say so I continued. "What is it? What's wrong?"

He sat up in the chair, now a little more eager to share his story. "I was over at the Taco Bell and the Virgin Mary came up to me and she gave me a Coke. Just about then, Jesus rode by on a Harley. "

I did not call his psychiatrist.

# Heroes: The Ultimate Love Story

*A hero is one who knows how*
*to hang on one minute longer.*

– Novalis (1772-1801)

The reputations of sports heroes tend to tarnish faster than silver wedding gifts. True heroes often shine, unheralded, in uncommon ways.

More than twenty years ago I was called in to see a woman named Debbie who had suffered brain damage during the birth of her twin son and daughter. She was now in a semi-conscious state. Her eyes were open, but her body seemed to be battling to find peace. She was biting her lower lip so severely that a large hole had opened between her lip and chin. She would grind her teeth, bite and moan helplessly.

Leo, Debbie's husband, and Bud, her father, met me at the hospital. I explained that my immediate concern was to protect her lip from further injury. Once we'd done that, we would address the teeth-grinding habit and tend to her other dental needs. Because she had no gag reflex, there was a risk of aspirating the dental materials, but with the assistance of a suction unit and skilled nurses, I anticipated no problems. Her family gave me permission to proceed.

First, we needed to take impressions of Debbie's teeth. We pried open her mouth, inserted the alginate trays, and succeeded in getting both an upper and a lower impression.

I had made two mouth guards for Debbie, similar to an athletic guard, from the same soft vacuum form that could be trimmed and adjusted at her bedside. Both fit well. The upper guard alone would not prevent her from rolling her lower lip over her bottom teeth and traumatizing her mouth. I asked that both guards be worn until her lip healed; then we would re-evaluate and decide whether wearing the lower one alone would protect her lip sufficiently.

I had perforated the guards and attached strings with safety pins that could be fastened to her garments; this would help us to retrieval the guards should she accidently choke on them. After trimming, smoothing and testing the guards several times, the time had come to introduce the nursing staff to Debbie's new appliances.

As a dentist you learn early not to put your fingers between a patient's teeth unless you use a prop to prevent inadvertent biting. I demonstrated how to work with the mouth guards without putting the staff's fingers at risk. The hard part was timing, because Debbie would not open her mouth upon command. It took some prying and oral stimulation to get her to open up.

Debbie wore the guards for about a week and during that time the soft tissue around her mouth healed nicely. But she continued to grind her teeth uncontrollably and without the guards she would traumatize her lip. I recommended that she wear only the lower guard to prevent permanent scarring.

With brain-injured patients it's impossible to predict whether such "bruxism" will decrease or increase with time. Any distress will increase para-functional activity. If Debbie chewed through the lower soft guard we would have to make her a hard one.

The next few weeks in the hospital did not produce the results we were hoping for. Nevertheless, Leo rearranged his life to make it possible to bring Debbie home. He also hired a personal attendant, which was the only way he could hope to cope with raising two babies, caring for his wife, and holding down a full-time job. Not many would have had the strength to handle this task.

Leo was also concerned with maintaining Debbie's dental health, so he asked me to come out to their home and demonstrate safe daily oral care.

IT WAS A SUNNY DAY as I walked to the front door of a modest home in a well-maintained Minneapolis suburb with mature trees and lovely gardens. Leo welcomed me in, and I was taken aback to see pictures of Debbie before the incident—on their wedding day, on vacations, doing the things young couples do as they await the arrival of their twins.

Leo, his father-in-law, Bud, and the personal attendant had created a hospital-like room on the first floor off the living room and equipped it with as much equipment as they could anticipate needing.

I withdrew from my black dental bag the aids I'd need to work on Debbie's mouth—tongue blades, mouth props, and a plastic wedge-like device to keep her from biting the tooth brush or their fingers. There was no standard routine that would apply here. It would be a process of trial and error to see what she would tolerate without struggle. Debbie was being tube-fed, so there was no food source for bacteria to produce acids leading to decay. She lacked the ability to swallow on command and there was a risk of oral fluids being aspirated into the lungs, so we tried to eliminate anything that could go down her throat. A suction unit periodically cleared her airway of secretions and saliva.

We had to simplify oral hygiene for Leo, who was still out of his comfort zone in personally caring for Debbie's needs in this department.

Bud and the personal attendant were to use the hard plastic device with one hand and a tooth brush in the other. It was impossible to safely train people to floss her teeth, so we compromised by dipping the tooth brush in chlorohexidrine with one hand and suctioning vigorously to prevent aspiration. This was not perfect, but it was something all caregivers could do while minimizing risks to Debbie and themselves.

We later transported Debbie into our office in a large reclined wheelchair for a more thorough cleaning and to determine if there were any dental problems we'd missed. We completed a thorough examination including radiographs and repaired some old, small cavities with the use of a mouth prop and a rubber dam.

As the years went by, Debbie's visits to our office became routine. Then one Monday evening, when she was with the hygienist for a routine cleaning and some bite-wing x-rays, the emergency light system suddenly went off.

The hygienist called out, "Debbie's got an x-ray film in her throat!"

I yelled, "Call 911!"

With no gag reflect to stop it, the film had slipped down. Debbie was laying back in the chair; her face was blue, her eyes were opened in a blank stare, but there were no breathing sounds. I depressed the back of her tongue with a dental mirror, but was unable to see anything. The Heimlich maneuver wouldn't work with gastric tubes in place, but I was able to tip her forward and establish an airway. As I held her body and supported her head, she immediately started to breathe and the pinkness came back to her face. The hygienist returned with the emergency kit and I was able to maintain the airway with Debbie's body position.

Our eighth-floor office is attached to a hospital with an emergency room, and I decided we would transport Debbie ourselves rather than waiting for an ambulance. With the hygienist driving the wheelchair, I maintained her airway successfully until we got her to the E.R..

I talked to the two physicians on duty while the hygienist returned with a copy of Debbie's chart from our office, and they took over her care. (Since that incident, if the patient is at risk of choking, we use a film holder or tie floss for easy retrieval.)

A few years after Debbie's brain injury, Leo took the case of Debbie's difficult delivery into court as a malpractice suit. The cost of around-the-clock care was staggering, and he struggled to consider an offer of 2.5 million dollars. At the advice of his counsel, he decided not to settle, lost the case and got nothing.

Leo took advantage of the great social services that the state of Minnesota has established. Ten years ago he suffered a heart attack, and he recently lost his job. But he has raised two fine children who grew up as unique, joyful adults. They have both graduated from college, his son as an artist and his daughter as a history major. She was married in a simple ceremony at home.

Leo remains a hero who created a fulfilling life that nurtured love and responsibility. No amount of money could have bought the rich gifts he brought to his family.

He and Debbie live in the same house, and he still talks about her as if they were twenty-year-old newlyweds.

He's the only living saint I've ever known.

# Oral Cancer Brings a Smile Back to a Mom

We are creatures of habit. We go through life repeating behaviors and interacting with people, while rarely getting to know them at all well. It may be the guy at the gas station or the lady at the drug store that we see often, but know very little about. Often you end up lumping them together with other people they remind you of, though the resemblances are often superficial and misleading.

That's what I did to the cashier at the drugstore in the professional building where I've worked for more than two decades. She's worked there for years but I never knew her name—until she became a patient of mine. I presumed she was not a happy lady because she never smiled. She would take her breaks outside so she could smoke. When I passed her in the halls she never greeted me with a hello. When I purchased something in the drugstore she never engaged in small talk or exchanges pleasantries. Her face was hard and her manner business-like. She seemed to be a reliable, hard working, and mind- your-own-business type of person.

One day a new patient was scheduled for intake procedures, which required that I review their medical and dental histories, complete an oral screening exam, check the patient's bite and also the temporal-mandible joint. Upon walking into the exam room I immediately recognized my new patient as the drugstore lady. It didn't surprise me that she sharing only the bare minimum of personal information required to complete her dental chart.

She had come to me on the recommendation of her son, who had joined our practice as a patient about a month earlier.

I found out that she was a widower in her early seventies with grown children. She had not been to the dentist for years, and knew that she had some dental needs. During the screening exam I noticed an ulceration on the lower left bony ridge right behind the second molar. I asked her how long that area had been sore? She told me that her doctor had advised her a year ago that he thought that might be a virus of some kind and recommended that she come back in two weeks if it didn't get better. I had a feeling she suspected the sore was cancerous and had waited as long as she could before coming in to find out.

You can't diagnose cancer without a biopsy, but based on her health history and the appearance of the lesion I was 99 percent sure that it was. I recommended that she see an oral surgeon as soon as possible for a biopsy. She balked, pointing out that she was here to see the dentist and wanted her teeth fixed. I replied as tactfully as I could that our choice of treatments would depend on the outcome of the biopsy.

The biopsy was positive for squamous cell carcinoma. The patient would require a radical neck procedure with a portion of her jaw bone being removed. She would only lose one tooth, but would have to undergo chemo and radiation.

The treatment of her cancer went well and we were able to restore her teeth. She will use prescription fluorides to help prevent decay in a very dry mouth. She lost one salivary gland from the radical neck procedure and the radiation affected the other major salivary gland.

The amazing thing her is her demeanor has changed dramatically as a result of all this medical intervention. She smiles when I see her in the halls. She is extremely pleasant when she visits the office. We talk about our kids and we share more about ourselves every time we have a chance. She is no longer the drugstore lady who distances herself from others, but now she is patient and a friend.

What has created such a change in her? Life? Death? What? The answer was Family. Her children were brought back into her life. As grown adults they had gone their own ways and had taken their mother's existence for granted. The cancer made her family unite and be grateful for all the hard work she had done for them. She finally felt acknowledged and appreciated.

As a parent you make many sacrifices for your children, and you do it out of love for those precious little ones. Children take their parents for granted and rarely understand all the time and resources that were devoted to their upbringing. Often it doesn't come home to roost until the children become parents themselves. She was lucky that cancer gave her family the push needed to verbalize their gratitude and appreciation.

# Family Stuff

## Going to Fly or Walk First?

Hoodwinked by her body changes into the thought that menopause had arrived, my mother gave my father the green light once too often, resulting in an unwanted surprise. Only a mother who has spent nine months nurturing it in the womb could love such an ugly unplanned baby, and it remained a distinct challenge for such a petite woman to expunge that ten-pound mistake from her womb. It was February of 1955 and I was that "oops" baby. At the time of my birth, my parents had experienced several potentially marriage-ending battles, survived droughts, floods, tornadoes and other natural disasters. The prospect of having yet another mouth to feed was not something they looked upon with relish.

Through out my life I was told that when I was born, my ears were so big that the family joke was: "Is he going to fly or walk first?"

Mom was so embarrassed by this late-in-life pregnancy that she avoided public display as if she had contracted leprosy. I was told that after she got to the point that she no longer could hide the belly bulge, she gathered the kids for an important family meeting. Mom proceeded to tell my brother Mike and my two sisters, Betty and Jo Ann, that she had a secret to share. "Mom is going to have a baby," she said, pointing at her stomach. "I do not want you to tell anybody yet."

My brother's innocent face became puzzled and he blurted out, "Can we tell Daddy?"

I have been flying ever since!

# The Valentine Ring

*I heard a good deal about a ring... but please... don't turn me into anything... unnatural.*

– J.R.R. Tolkien, *The Lord of the Rings*

Many Valentine Days have come and gone with few memorable expressions of my unwavering love for my wife. I am romantically challenged—not unusual for a man who has been married for almost thirty-two years.

As I reflect on the past, seeking inspiration for this year's symbol of admiration, a journey of perfection traveled even before we were married springs to mind.

I was a dental student in Lincoln, Nebraska, searching for someone to engrave my hand-made Valentine's Day ring for Lynne. It was a gold ring with a setting in the shape of a simple heart. To make it a perfect gift, I wanted it personalized with the letter "L."

None of the jewelry and department stores I contacted were willing to take on the liability of engraving this custom-made ring, and by February 13th, my desperation was growing.

At last, my search sent me down a lonely side street to an old store-front with a modest sign centered above it: John's Trophy Shop. Inside, the showroom displayed figurines large and small, plaques, trophies of gold and silver, wooden and plastic, elegant and tacky, all lying-in-wait for the next champion of whatever.

A voice yelled, "I'm back here!"

John, a middle-aged man in fraying blue jeans and t-shirt, sat with a magnifying glass strapped to his sandy-gray head, humped over a precious trophy in progress, holding pieces together by hand, waiting for the glue to dry.

He peered out, "I'll be with you as soon as this crap finally sets up."

The silence and a feeling of comfortable disorganization stood in stark contrast to the mall stores where I'd been searching for my coveted engraver. The dim, dusty working area was cluttered with tools lying haplessly here and there, and the most recent grindings were piled under an old wooden stool, but John could reach any tool he wanted from his perch. It seemed as if I were viewing the inner soul of a skilled craftsman, cocooned in comfortable contentment with his beloved occupation.

John finally straightened up with a smile and deep, penetrating blue eyes. "What brings you to the shop?"

I quickly retrieved the ring from my pocket and handed it to him. "I cast this ring and was wondering if you could engrave the letter 'L' on the face of the heart."

"For your wife?"

"No, it's for the girl friend."

He flipped down his magnifying glasses and inspected it. "You do a lot of casting?"

"I'm in dental school. We're casting crowns and inlays for our patients, and we also make jewelry for fun."

He motioned with his head to follow him to the other end of the room, where he carefully clamped the ring into his engraving unit.

"I play around with castings, too," he said. "Yea, last summer, I poured molten silver over a plate of spaghetti and let it set. Then I flipped it over, polished some selective areas, attached it to a wooden plaque and won first prize at the Nebraska State Fair."

He engraved the ring, chuckling like a small child who just got away with something.

"What else have you waxed by hand other than teeth?"

I paused while he was undoing the ring from the clamp. He handed it to me; the engraved "L" was perfect.

"What do I owe you for that?"

"The conversation will do."

He smiled. Clearly he derived his joy largely from his craftsmanship, with monetary success a secondary concern.

That was back in the late seventies. Looking back on that incidental event, I hit upon the perfect idea for a Valentine's gift. Instead of adorning my wife with yet one more piece of professional cookie-cutter jewelry, I would dig into her jewelry box and retrieve that old heart ring. I hope it will remind her of our early love.

But just in case it doesn't, maybe I'll buy a back-up gem, returnable. Or change the sheets on the sofa bed in the basement.

## Fishing for Wisdom

*Many men go fishing all of their lives without knowing that it is not fish they are after.*

– Henry David Thoreau

My dad's northern Saskatchewan fishing camp immersed us in an undisturbed natural world near the earth's most northern ice cap, worlds away from all responsibility.

The site was so far north, the trees were stunted cousins of the ones I was familiar with back home in Iowa. There were no roads in this remote part of the bush—float planes and canoes were the only way in or out. On the short, 70-mile flight to Lake Jewitt, the landscape below the plane's windows appeared to be more water than land.

Once we'd disembarked and the plane disappeared again into the sky, we were completely cut off from the rest of the world. There were no radios or phones to communicate with anyone outside our camp. We were at the mercy of the charter schedule, dependent on the plane's return at a pre-arranged timeline. That lack of connection could be dangerous if someone became ill or was injured, but it was also extremely liberating. Day-to-day worry became non-existent.

The crude one-room cabin was nestled in the northern-most lake region of Saskatchewan. The cabin had been commissioned by the nearby air charters for hunting moose, but it had been built by the indigenous Cree people. They had framed the walls and the bunk beds with small, debarked pine trees and uninsulated plywood.

The cabin's exterior was a feeble barrier to the Canadian cold, but we kept the numerous drafts at bay by tending a small, black pot-bellied stove day and night. As a result, the cabin was usually too hot when the stove was stoked up, and too cold when we let the fire die down. The green, tar-paper roof kept the place relatively dry and served as a visual landmark for the incoming pilots.

As the groan of the departing float plane vanished into the breeze, a quiet spirit of peace descended upon us and we embraced our isolation. Whatever tasks we had left behind would just have to wait until we returned.

And each year I returned to the place, the decompression time got shorter, and I found it easier to "let go." Soon the cobwebs of my brain would clear and I would be free from anything remotely worldly.

Our schedule for opening up the cabin was a crap shoot; it was largely dependent on when the ice went out, which varied considerably from year to year. The plane needed open water to land safely and the ice had to be clear in front of the cabin so we could unload the spring's extra large load. Phone calls were exchanged with the Canadian locals and coordinated with the ending of the our kids' high school year.

In exchange for the lifetime lease for the cabin, Dad, my older brother, Mike, and I painted the flight charter's hotel, restaurant, cabins and private home. One short, mid-summer week of labor from the three of us allowed Dad to own his private paradise in the Canadian wilderness.

We usually arrived in the region in mid-June when the waters were still covered with what the locals called "black ice," a condition that occurred just before it disappeared. We typically spent a couple of nights in the cabins at the Thompson Camp, waiting anxiously for the ice to go as we transferred the cargo from our extra-large van into the Twin Otter plane.

Thompson first loaded the plane with a number of red, twenty-gallon barrels of gas and several silver propane tanks. The crew then did its best not to exceed the plane's maximum legal weight limits while accommodating my dad's annual spending spree on boat motors, propane refrigerator, new propane stove jets, fishing equipment galore, foam cushions for the plywood slat beds, more tar paper (always needed), chainsaws, ice picks and tongs, rain gear, dry foods, supply coolers, boxes of canned foods, shot guns and ammunition, an assortment of miscellaneous hardware, and several boxes of 12 x 12 vinyl flooring.

The pilot and crew carefully balanced the load to insure that the plane could safely take off and land. During the flight we sat on the gas barrels.

Once we were up in the air cruising toward Jewett Lake, we were mesmerized by the seemingly endless expanse of water and land moving by below us. After a while it all began to look the same to us, and we were amazed that the pilot was able to navigate flawlessly into camp.

We had come to expect all sorts of damage due to the harsh winter, but each year our first glimpse of the cabin from the air gave us a rough assessment of what condition it was in. Typically, the winter ice crushed the boat dock into shreds. The plane was usually forced to straddle the shoreline for that first trip. But this year, as we motored across the lake, my dad called out proudly, "My dock made through the winter!"

But as we got closer, we realized that a new dock had been constructed. The pine beams were much thicker than the ones we used and the saw-cuts were fresh. Had someone built Dad a new dock? In any case, the pilot was relieved that his floats would be spared a rocky landing, and Dad and I were happy to have the chore of rebuilding the dock out of the way.

We quickly unloaded the plane and the pilot taxied across the lake, so he could take off directly into the wind. We watched the aircraft disappear over the horizon to the east. We were now on our own for a week. The cabin and the grounds begged for us to open up for a new year.

We pried the plywood off the windows and doors, entered the cabin and found a note conspicuously placed on the dining table, "I used your cabin while I was trapping. I also used some of your gas for my snowmobiles. Thank you for everything and I built you a new dock as payment for the gas. Tom Looking Bear."

We had just learned the native's code of honesty in the bush. The men who survive out here trap all winter long and work as fishing guides during the summer months. If they're discovered to be dishonest, they're shunned by the tribe and forced to leave the area. People know who's out in the bush and where they're going. It's hard to hide when there are so few people around to begin with.

Dad and I hustled about trying to get the long list of chores behind us. We fetched pails of water for the kitchen and the hand washing station—a large white bowl with a bar of soap and a towel from home. We changed out some of the old propane lanterns, replacing the mantels. We cut foam mats for the beds, changed the propane tanks, switched on the stove jets, stocked the kitchen, and chopped and stacked wood for the potbelly stove.

We felt like true pioneers as we cut large chunks of ice from the creek beds which feed the lake, loaded them in the boats, and transported them back to camp. We dug down to the bottom of the log ice house, dumped in the ice, covered it with the saw dust, and then sealed off the door with tar paper.

We replaced the fiberglass bottoms on a couple of old boats, changed out sparkplugs and started up all the Mercury outboards. My dad had bought some huge Zebco replacement reels and thick fiberglass rods he nicknamed "broom handles." We rigged the rod and reels and packed the tackle boxes with new leaders, doctor and professor spoons.

Then we swept out the place. The floor was bare, worn plywood, but we had brought boxes of self-sticking 12 x 12 vinyl tiles to class it up. Laying the tile was not a priority this trip, but if we got bored, it could happen.

All the while, the cold, blue waters of the lake beyond the camp, dissected here and there by the gray irregular rocky shores, reflected the bright blue sky and left us breathless in awe.

TWO MILLION YEARS AGO, glaciers began to advance and retreat from the polar icecap in a seemingly endless cycle that repeatedly scoured the touch igneous surfaces of the Canadian Shield and left the region's earth, rocks, lakes, rivers, trees and creatures with a mystic aura. All seemed to be random, yet it possessed a glorious and serene construction engineered by a slow evolution of the great mother earth and blessed by the Almighty. As time passed at the camp, we would become attuned to this serene and dramatic history, and we'd also begin to pick up the sounds that might have escaped our ears in a more hectic setting. The wind danced through the trees with swishes of swaying leaves, the call of a lone loon and screeching sounds of new babies in the nearby eagle's nest. In the darkness of night, the scream of a lynx across the water resembled the distress call of a woman.

We could taste the fresh purity and the true cleanliness of the air, though in time it became polluted with our own intrusions—the smoke from the wood stove, the smell of fried bacon, spilled gasoline, un-bathed males, the nearby outhouse, sudsy dish water toss off into the brush, and other casual disposals.

On the lake, the fresh fragrance of clean cold water was foreign to my senses. From a distance each shoreline appeared alike. With the confusing maze of its repetitive shapes and sizes the lake could become mesmerizing to a novice, though a seasoned veteran recognized the various islands and bays and spot the subtle idiosyncrasies in the landscape that would guide him back home.

I thought back to the Seventies when my dad had invited me to go fishing with his retiree friends. At the time my father was in his sixties; I was eighteen years old and assumed he had brought me along as their "go-for" or youthful grunt.

Back then, I was just like my daughter is now—not a willing or a receptive audience to a father's wisdom—and my father knew it. At the time I would be more willingly to accept random advice from complete strangers.

Dad had booked us with five of his Alcoholics Anonymous buddies who were in their seventies and eighties. It was a twenty-four-hour drive in an extended cargo van to the landing strip where we were to catch the Beaver float plane. I did most of the night driving and when we loaded the plane I did the lion's share of the work. I thought the old guys were using me as a labor whore, though as the trip progressed each one of them shared their personal secrets, unique gifts and prophetic words of wisdom. The personal experience of fatherhood has reinforced a notion I dimly glimpsed even then: I was not at camp for the fish or the labor. I was there to inherit the wisdom from the wounded. Dad took me along hoping that I would gain some insights from him and his old cronies.

But the primary focus of our visit was fishing. As the guests anxiously prepared their fishing gear, Dad and I raced to get the boats and motors floating. The fishing boats were made of heavy wooden slats and had bench seats. They were twenty feet long, and could handle the winds and waves that sometimes came up unexpected on the expansive lake, though it took four men to carry them from storage to the water. We gassed up the motors and cautioned the guests not to wander too far afield unless they were sure they knew the way back.

During that week of fishing and conversation, I got to know Dad's friends pretty well. Gus, my first fishing mate, was a wealthy eighty-three-year-old retired grain elevator operator. He was tall and thin man with a full head of snow-white hair and sported a full handled-bar mustache. His uniform for the week consisted of thick red flannel shirts, tightly belted blue jeans and a red "DeKalb" baseball cap.

Gus proudly told me that he was the financial genius of the group and despite life's troubles he had managed and hang onto most of his wealth over the years. He had hunted big game and fished all parts of North America, but had lost contact with his family due to years of uncontrolled drinking. "I was just not there for my family when they needed me."

His story was that of financial discipline and wealth accumulation by the simple concept of paying yourself first. Sadly, his was not a story of happiness, but a long lonely life of greed. He taught me that when you reach the end of your life and find that your family no longer wants to be a part of it, things can seem very shallow. "I was too stingy, not only with my money, but also with my heart."

Harold was a retired finish carpenter who had recently befriended my father. He was very competitive and could readily pile on the BS. Though he was a recovered alcoholic, he talked about his past escapades with pride rather than remorse, even though his behavior had often been despicable. He had even spent a couple of years in jail for manslaughter, but he seemed proud of it. Harold had a grandiose self image and spoke as if the world revolved around him. He wore bib overalls all week and a lit cigarette seemed permanently attached to the left side of his mouth.

I spent a boorish day listening to Harold's self-professed accomplishments and came away appreciating the quiet quality of humility. Unfortunately, when I was with Harold we did catch the biggest fish and did not hear the end of that all week long. He was a lonely man.

Hank was the odd duck in the group. He was an extremely shy old man and wore an ugly toupee all week even though he was with a group of men who never bathed. It seemed as if he was invited mostly out of pity. He was a man of multiple careers, married with no children and literally a man of few words. Whatever he shared was always calculated.

Hank lived an unremarkable life, working as a mechanic and married to the same woman for thirty years. Then one morning he woke up to find that his wife had passed in her sleep. He described that day as the most stunningly disappointing day of his life. She was the reason he lived. She was the reason he had quit drinking. He never wanted to lose her. He was truly a quiet romantic. He always expected that he would die first, so he had never planned for this in his life. He was lost. He tried to cope by returning to the bottle, but his relapse didn't help.

Marge, a widow who lived next door, started to help take care of him. He was content since his wife would have approved of her. They eventually got married, that his love for his first wife remained the driving force of his life, even in his second marriage.

Charlie, a retired heavy machinery operator, was the salt of the earth. He was a hard-working construction worker who seemed to treasure the simple life. He was a smoker and drinker, and coughed and hacked all week long. He was self-abusive in many ways. He ate like crap and did not seem to care for himself. His health reflected his poor habits. Once when I was out in the boat with him he suffered a coughing jag that seemed endless, and I feared for his life.

In short, Charlie was a poster child for poor health. I was guessing Charlie was brought along to show me what bad habits can do to a man in the course of a few decades.

Tom was a short, balding red-headed Irishman who once owned a lumber supply company and had been through several marriages. He was a guy's guy who was perplexed when it came to relationships with women and acknowledged his total ignorance of the female gender.

It seems he was an excellent father but a terrible husband. He thought his wife would love him if he treated the kids well, but extended far less affection in her direction. Both of his parents drank, and he made promises to himself that he would avoid that path, but the alcoholic bug bit him hard a couple times. His wife moved on, but his kids stayed by his side, and he would do anything for them. My dad could relate with Tom. Sober, both could be great men.

On the last day of our trip, Dad shared with me how AA and the twelve-step program had allowed him to maintain his sobriety, and expounded his theory of why men drink uncontrollably. "A man will not be comfortable in his own shoes until he lives the life that he thought that his mother would want him to live. Once he is able to accomplish that feat, then he'll be able to tolerate his own skin."

I challenged him, "You cannot tell me that if you and I shared a beer, you'd become an alcoholic again." He looked up into the clouds, rubbed his chin and replied, "No, I cannot tell you that. But it is not worth it for us to find out."

Finally, he got around to discussing my career or vocation. He shared his personal disappointment with his own journey. "My uncle Clem was a large-animal vet and he went to Canada for his education. They were poor immigrant farmers, but he became a respected professional. I would loved to have been a vet. Education was the ticket off the farm. But the Depression hit and took away my college chances. To help support Mom and the younger kids, I slaughtered cattle on the hoof.

"You can count on me to help pay for your college. I want you to take full advantage of it and not look back with any regrets."

Last year Dad flew in a couple of aluminum boats that we positioned on the far side of portages to Hollingshead and Hill lakes. The northern pike were hitting faster than ever. I still treasure the memory.

# My Perfect Dentures

Although I'm a dentist, my father eschewed wearing his dentures.

In an era prior to the advent of dental implants, his insatiable sweet tooth ultimately left him in a condition that I would describe as "a dentally handicapped."

For the surgical extraction of his natural teeth and the insertion of his first set of oral dread, he was hospitalized in St. Vincent Hospital in Sioux City for a couple of days.

Back in the 1960s, children were considered to be teeming with infectious bugs, so I was only allowed to visit my father's hospital window, where he reassured me with a wave of recognition, a thumbs up, and his new, awkward smile.

Over the years he often forgot where he had left the dentures, and undertook many desperate treasure hunts, often just before the arrival of "company." Mom, Dad and the four kids all searched the mostly likely locations: between the driver's car seat cushions, in the bathroom's yellow soaking cup, in the top drawer of the desk next to his green upholstered TV chair, on the rim of the kitchen sink and atop the hand-stitched needlepoint doily on the dresser next to his bed.

After we had looked everywhere and come up empty-handed, my father would walk into the house with a big toothy smile.

"I found them. They were in my mouth the whole time."

At first, he only wore his store-bought teeth when he was in the public eye. Once his social obligations ended, he would immediately remove the despised choppers, and his secret covey was tucked away in the back of his dresser drawer.

My mother was a veteran denture wearer; we never saw her without her pearly whites. She had no sympathy for my father's laundry list of complaints and would mercilessly attack what remained of his personal vanity with insulting words of shame.

"Ted, without your teeth, your mouth looks like a 'butt hole'." A rising sense of futility would finally bring her tireless but ineffectual nagging to an end.

My father, after all, was a stubborn pudgy Irishman who no longer thought that missing teeth would interfere with his acceptance in his limited social circle. He learned to chew most foods on the naked boney ridges, so he only used false teeth as a sporadic vanity appliance.

Who knows if that lively banter may have influenced my choice of a career?

After four years of dental school and a few years of professional experience, I was confident that I could make my father a "perfect denture." I felt as if I owed it to him, since he had worked hard and made sacrifices to give me twelve years of private parochial education, an undergraduate education, and the further opportunity to complete a graduate degree in Dental Surgery.

I invited him up for the week and asked him to bring his collection of failures, hoping I could learn from them. When he arrived for my welcomed payback, he unceremoniously dumped the pile of dentures on the counter top. I paired the uppers with the lowers, matching them by the color and texture of the old acrylic appliances. I picked up the ones he called the old Honkers.

"That set was just too big. It rubbed my mouth sore everywhere."

The Honkers had overextended the peripheral borders, but I assumed my father failed to have the peripheral borders adequately adjusted by the dentist, so he would develop sores if worn for even a short period of time. Most men don't understand the adjustment process around dentures, so they only give us a limited chance to make things right before they discount our credibility and quit on us. My father must have quit early with the dentist who made the Honkers.

The next set I picked up my father called the Bombers. "They were so small and loose," he informed me, "that they would drop out of my mouth like bombs. They were made by that ninety-year old dentist in Yankton for a couple hundred bucks."

This set was under-extended and the teeth were too small for my father's face. It was a comfort denture, but lacked adequate retention.

"The Clackers," my dad shared, "were the last set I had made, and they fit the best of the bunch, but when I would try to speak with them in my mouth they would 'clack' together. It drove me crazy."

That left one set, the first he had owned. "I wore my first set the longest, but once, when I was pouring a seamless flooring system, the chemicals permeated my dentures. They tasted like polyurethane and that's when I finally gave up. Your mother made me try all these dentists, and they made an attempt to make something that would work for me. I know you can do it."

Several impressions, perfect records, ideal teeth were selected, wax try-in, small alterations, counseling, encouragement and little gratitude left us at the point of the perfect denture. They "fit" and they looked good. Mom and Dad both left smiling. She was happy to see her husband joining normal civilization again and he was proud of the job I did. Talking with them would take some practice, however, since my father needed to get used to having all that stuff in his mouth again. I knew he would need a while to adjust to them.

Months later we went home to visit the folks for Thanksgiving and dad greeted us with a big smile revealing that he was proudly wearing his dentures. But when he attempted to speak, his garbled words immediately tipped me off that he was wearing his perfect dentures as if I were "company."

"Dad, you don't have to wear the dentures on my account. Please take them out so we can talk." With relief, his teeth came out and his toothless smile again took on a sense of warm normalcy. He was Dad again and not my professional failure.

Despite his fatherly love and his personal pride of my accomplishments, "My son's last ditch effort" got filed deep in his secret drawer.

They were used on one further occasion, for his last public appearance lying lifelessly in his casket.

"Doesn't he look good!" was repeated again and again by the attendees at his funeral.

Oddly enough, I derived a sense of both pride and closure knowing that he was buried with my perfect dentures.

# "Shit"

I was listening to Frank McCourt's audio book *Angela's Ashes* and his use of the word "shit" struck me as familiar. I suddenly realized why my own life has been similarly plagued with such impropriety. My father's family is Irish, one hundred per cent.

My Irish grandmother Young's family hosted a reunion in Wakonda, South Dakota, many years ago. At this event an array of shirt-tail, lace-curtain relatives celebrated life with jokes, stories, food, and more than a little beer.

My sister arrived from Indiana, and once she'd introduced her teenagers to our father's relatives the use of the word "shit" became so commonplace they called it "The Shit Reunion."

That was when it dawned on me that the prevalence of the word in family conversations must have its roots in a shared culture. Like it or not, it was part of my Irish heritage.

My Norwegian mother repeatedly reminded me that my first childhood sentence was, "Oh shit! I broke it."

The Catholic school grammar system attempted to erase this tendency. Soapy mouths, whacked hands, paddled behinds and endless pages of "I will not cuss or swear in school" all failed to end my habit.

The high school wrestling coach who headed up the Young Christian Athlete Organization never invited me to join because my uncontrollable tongue convinced him that I must also lack the required faith.

Summer jobs working for commercial painting and construction contractors alongside a bunch of macho males did nothing to temper my early-life verbal imprinting. Not only did they accept my blue speech, but they expanded my vocabulary to new and even less savory areas—areas of vernacular so disgusting that I could only imagine that I was becoming well-prepared for the conversations I was sure to have in Hell.

The true test of restraint came when I entered dental school. Years of spontaneous eruptions had to be curtailed under the auspices of being a professional.

No one would go to a dentist who would remove the drill from a patient's mouth and say, "Oh shit! I broke it."

# The Ferris Wheel

*I see nothing in space as promising as*
*the view from a Ferris wheel.*

– E. B. White

My dating experience as an adolescent was like a small child touching a hot stove. Regardless of my intellect and hoards of advice from my older brother not to touch, I always seemed to end up with my ego burnt.

My boyish desire for a girl to "like me" drove me to behave irrationally during that dreaded mating season of life. The painful memories of personal acts of stupidity, my complete ignorance of women and their mysterious needs still haunt my male machismo.

The reference above to the Ferris wheel, by one of my favorite humorists, uses the word "promising." I'd like to replace it with "humiliating."

When we were teenagers, a buddy and his girl arranged a blind date with her best friend. They thought we would make the perfect couple, and plans were set for us to attend the South Dakota State Fair.

The fair was in full swing and our date progressed cordially as we enjoyed Pronto Pups, snow cones and mountainous pink clouds of cotton candy. She was impressed with my skills playing the games of the Midway's arcade. I took pride in winning trinkets and keepsakes with which she could adorn her beautiful body. They would also serve as mementos of our perfect first date. We did seem meant for each other.

The infatuation was untarnished until it came time to decide which rides we'd experience together. She loved the rides that spun endlessly and I liked the ones that went high. I loved roller coasters, sky rockets, Ferris wheels, and rides that went up and down; but I couldn't handle the ones that spun. She hated heights, but delighted in becoming dizzy—an effect that in my world often crossed the threshold into motion sickness. It was the first test to our budding relationship. She insisted that she needed to spin, and to please her, I reluctantly acquiesced. The trade-off was that after I went on the Scrambler with her, she'd go on the Ferris wheel with me.

The Scrambler was just what I expected; the thrust and spins pushed our hot bodies crushingly together as we whirled around and around. I would have enjoyed being rhythmically pressed up against this young woman if it were not for the revolt taking place in my stomach.. I exited the ride looking and feeling green with motion sickness. As we proceeded to my preferred ride, I was trying desperately not to reveal how horrible I felt.

We joined the couples lining up under the massive Ferris wheel's bright lights and multicolored splendor and before long we were strapped in the rocking seats, cheek to cheek. There was not an empty car as the wheel began to rotate high into the cool, dark evening skyline.

Suddenly, just as we hovered over the love birds below us, my stoic self-control exploded, showering heads, clothes—anything exposed to my line of fire. Great groans of disgust issued from the unlucky victims below.

Of course, there was no goodnight kiss that night, and my ego was too fried to attempt any recovery from that regretful first date. But life is learning, and sometimes it takes some spins on a Scrambler to really get that lesson across.

# Endless Perfect Ice

We would skate all winter long above the old grain-milling dam on the frozen Vermillion River, which meandered lazily along the western edge of Centerville, South Dakota.

Every year we anxiously waited for the first cold spell to hit. Once Old Man Winter arrived to stay, he would miraculously create the thickness of ice required for a parental green light to skate. From that point on, the skating season proceeded non-stop, with episodes of heavy snowfall and the rapid fall of darkness only temporarily impeding our countless skating adventures.

A bridge crossed the river northwest of town along the route to "The Old Beach" and Gunderson Park, and its spans kept the frozen river beneath it free of snow. We played hockey there on a largely imaginary rink, using scrap wood for hockey sticks and tin cans for pucks. Many a Stanley Cup championship was decided on that secret, sheltered frozen oasis.

Most of the time we were kept warm by the sweat of our battles, but occasionally we stoked up a fire on the river's edge fueled by the ample supply of driftwood that lined the ancient river.

Leftover Christmas cookies and thermoses filled with hot chocolate were freely shared, so we could play until we dropped. Boys and girls, young and old were all welcomed into our ever-hopeful hockey dynasties. In some years, when snowfall was limited or we were feeling a little more industrious, we would shovel a clearing on the ice behind our Centerville house, which was perched on the eastern shores of the river. The advantage of this arrangement was that our kitchen could act as both the warming house and the snack bar, even though Dad had just installed a fresh new linoleum floor. Thanks, Mom.

One cold "snowless" winter in the 1960s, nature blessed the meandering Vermillion with an endless sheet of perfectly smooth and pristine ice, tempting us to embark on a cross-county skating adventure.

The enticement to explore was irresistible, and one day my older brother, Mike, and I, with two other willing explorers, excitedly set off heading north along the meandering river into uncharted territory. The decision to follow this frozen highway was a spur-of-the-moment thing, and it never occurred to us to get permission, pack supplies, or even tell our families where we were going. We skated and skated on the winding and the wildly snaking river across the farmlands north of town, looking back from time to time at the royal blue cylindrical water tower and the church steeples of the town we were rapidly leaving far behind us. The feeling of immense freedom, the changing landscapes, the novelty and the borderless track fueled our desire to thoughtlessly press on. Around each bend a new vista, a new experience came into view. We meandered under old steel bridges, past country cemeteries, open springs, majestic industrial farms, and crumbling rural homesteads, many of them abandoned. We passed under high cliffs, through thick, cottonwood groves, and across sections of wide open flat plains, following in the footsteps of the early settlers who had coveted the river-bottom land for its fertility and also its easy access to drinking water.

Late on that glorious day, the four of us took up the challenge of a spur-of-the-moment testosterone-driven race that ended abruptly when we came unexpected upon a string of barbed wire strung across the ice from bank to bank at just below knee level. We were all slammed violently to the ice, though the fall was cushioned by our thick winter coats, hats and gloves. We found ourselves skidding across the velvety smooth frozen surface and began to laugh hysterically at our ungainly transit. Once we'd gathered up our slightly wounded bodies, we noticed that the sun was about to set. We were several miles from town by that time, and we debated whether it would be faster to retrace our path down the meandering river or take off our skates and walk back to town via a more direct cross-country route.

In our infinite state of novice wisdom we decided to walk. A few hundred yards of cold stocking feet on rock-hard plowed fields quickly convinced us we'd made a mistake. We returned to the river, put our skates back on, and began another race—this time against the darkness—that we knew we could never win.

We finally arrived back home well after dark, to be greeted by fierce tongue lashings and threats of dire punishment, few of which were administered. Even if they had been, it would have been a small price to pay for that once-in-a-lifetime afternoon of boundless adventure and sheer joy on the boundless river ice.

## Life's Treasure Chest

*God grant me the serenity to accept the things I cannot change, courage to change the things I can, and wisdom to know the difference.*

– Reinhold Niebuhr, The Serenity Prayer

A massive walnut box, known by my family as "the desk," was the treasure chest that graced the heart of my boyhood home. It was an old, scratched and a much-worn piece, but our most important family documents were squirreled away in its drawers and the desk invited the whole family to the fruits of its treasure.

A clunky black telephone, our only conduit to the outside world, was either perched on top of the desk or neatly placed beside it on the gold metal phone table. The whole family rifled through the drawers at one time or another, searching for their own current life's nugget, which always seemed to be filed somewhere within the depths of this bottomless ocean of scattered papers.

There were cherished keepsakes from years past mixed in with malfunctioning pens, broken pencils, and straight-edge rulers emblazoned with the logos of paint manufacturers. The drawers accommodated tax forms, birth certificates, deeds, business contacts, phone books, vacation mementoes, paper, pens, pencils and a myriad of office supplies that we all needed to navigate throughout our school life; and piles of my dad's Alcoholics Anonymous (AA) propaganda also filled the over-stuffed drawers. He had been cursed with the personal demon of alcoholism.

Above the desk was a wall plaque with "The Serenity Prayer" hung permanently at eye level. Those words were omnipresent, and they helped my father maintain the mental strength to avoid "falling off the wagon."

> God grant me the serenity
> to accept the things I cannot change;
> courage to change the things I can;
> and wisdom to know the difference.
> Living one day at a time;
> Enjoying one moment at a time;
> Accepting hardships as the pathway to peace;
> Taking, as He did, this sinful world
> as it is, not as I would have it;
> Trusting that He will make all things right
> if I surrender to His Will;
> That I may be reasonably happy in this life
> and supremely happy with Him
> Forever in the next.
> Amen.
>
> – *Reinhold Niebuhr*

I spent hours at the desk, on the phone or working on my homework, and I must have read the inscription a million times. The prayer became so ingrained in my unconscious thought patterns that it never occurred to me until recently that it has guided me throughout my life.

For example, I've always accepted the fact that crisis is a fact of life, not a punishment. I interpreted the lines, "Accepting hardships as the pathway to peace," by viewing crisis as an opportunity for change. "Enjoying one moment in time," underscores the reality of my daily existence. I make an effort to remain present and seldom take  the here-and-now for granted.

"Living one day at a time." I realized early in my practice as a dentist that when a patients come in with feelings of shame or guilt about their past oral hygiene negligence, there's no use in being judgmental. We can't change yesterday, nor can we control our tomorrows. We can only deal with life where we are right now.

We have all been given talents and intellect. The most difficult task described in the prayer might be the self-examination required to differential between the things we can and can't change. Who are we, really? What is our potential? What are our limits?

Success comes from living up to your potential and beyond. Happiness comes from the wisdom that you are living close to your maximum potential and the faith in God that He will make you supremely happy for eternity. Unknowingly, I've had faith that He will make things right.

After many years of twelve-step calls as part of my father's dedication to AA, he developed an armchair Freudian observation of male alcoholics that went something like this: "A man will not be happy with himself until he lives a life he thinks that his mother would want him to live."

Three years before I was born, my father found AA and that Serenity. Thankfully his prayer found me.

## Grandma Bergina's Kitchen

*A house is not a home unless it contains*
*food and fire for the mind as well as the body.*

– Margaret Fuller

My Norwegian grandmother Bergina's butter was always home-churned, never store bought. Her eighty-year-old, arthritic hands perfectly blended its homegrown flavor. Whenever the sweet flavor of "real" butter crosses my taste buds, melted into a heavenly slurry on a slice of warm, freshly-baked bread, I savor the smooth, light-yellow smear, with the subtle hint of salt. It sends me back to my grandmother's South Dakota kitchen.

The homestead was nestled between the small towns of Volin and Mission Hill, South Dakota, in a remote patch of Missouri River bottomland countryside chosen for its rich, black-soiled fields. The farmhouse kitchen held a gigantic white range fueled mainly by the previous year's waste, recycled from the corn harvest on the great muddy. The massive cast-iron wood stove nearby served as a tireless belly of energy for baking, cooking, heating pails of hand-carried water, and heating the drafty pioneer farmhouse itself.

When the round, cast-iron portholes on the oven's flat top were cracked opened, the dancing spews of flames shot out like a prehistoric dragon breathing fire. When not stoked up for cooking, it emitted a blanket of toasty warmth that enveloped the kitchen.

The kitchen was both the home's working center and the place where the family gathering for mental and physical replenishment during those long, hard days of farm labor. Family members and guests would seat themselves on the high rib-backed chairs encircling the expansive oak table in the center of the room, invariably covered with an oil cloth.

My uncles would keep the wood box filled with dried corn cobs, adding occasional scraps of wood or split logs. But it was Grandma who skillfully devised the perfect mix of cobs and wood to suit the current task at hand or social gathering. I can still sense the love that emanated from her humped-back body as she shuffled about the kitchen on the thread-bare linoleum floor.

I still marvel at the array of smells and flavors of the many savory delicacies she was able to produce by means of such rudimentary equipment. Many of her techniques had been passed on to her from preceding generations, no doubt, though I'm sure she also developed quite a few of her own during her years in that kitchen. Cookbooks and electrical appliances were not a part of the formula.

When not in use, the stainless-steel milk separator stood in the corner next to the kitchen's walk-in pantry like a noble adornment to the tabernacle of my grandmother's mysterious culinary arts. She had cleaned it impeccably, time and again, with her loving, age-spotted hands and it gleamed like a shrine.

The milk, hand-milked each morning by my bachelor uncles—Clarence, Alfred and Harold—came from a small herd of brown-and-white patched Herefords that were allowed to graze freely in the pasture, their diet supplemented occasionally by last year's hay and crib-stored corn. The rich variety of grasses they enjoyed gave the cows' milk, and the butter churned from it, a special sweetness, just as clover flowers sweeten the honey of industrious bees.

I cannot recall a single instant when my grandmother referred to a note card or a cookbook. The masterpieces she produced almost daily had been seared into her memory over the course of decades at the stove. My mother revered her mother's skills, though she didn't possess them to the same degree herself. The contrast left her with lifelong feelings of inadequacy, envy, and even jealousy, though it was the result of faulty logic to some degree. My mother reasoned that there could be only *one* master of such challenging culinary arts in a household, and her own mother was it.

Lefse took on the roll of the "Holy Grail" of that Old Norwegian's kitchen. My mother sought out every technique and tool, including rollers, flat irons and electric flat plates. The results were good, but neither the taste nor the texture or color of the end product ever quite measured up to my grandmother's exquisitely crafted creations.

My grandmother had been given an unwelcome head start on the path to becoming our homesteader queen matriarch. In 1893 her own mother died of scarlet fever. She was twelve at the time.

I have gleaned from her conversations as an adult that as a child my mother was obsessed with gender-based cultural delineations of household roles and duties. I get the impression that she watched and listened to her own mother like an acolyte, eager to pick up the slightest hints of domestic technique or maternal wisdom that might fall from her mother's lips like crumbs from a table.

One spring Sunday afternoon after a family gathering, we were driving out of Grandma's meager farmyard on the weed-lined gravel driveway. As an eight year old "city" kid, I turned to my mother and asked, "Is Grandmother poor?"

My mother quickly returned, "No, Grandma's not poor; she's Norwegian."

I think back on that exchange today, as I savor the taste of "real" butter on warm bread.

# Harold's Gift

My father's painting crew crowded around our kitchen table most mornings, swigging down copious cups of coffee, discussing job assignments, analyzing progress reports, trouble-shooting, and planning for the day ahead. Our whole family joined in while we ate breakfast and packed our school lunches at the same table. It was truly a mom and pop shop.

Harold was a workhorse on the crew, but he was plagued throughout his life with an irresistible urge to drink. My father admired and treasured Harold's ability to outwork three able-bodied men while sober, and he also bragged behind his back that Harold had been the valedictorian of his high school class.

Harold was a good-looking man, tall, trim and muscular, with a polite charm. His jet-black hair was neatly combed, side-parted and glistening with hair cream. His clothes were crisp, well-pressed and neatly tucked in. When I was a small boy, I marveled at his shiny shoes, and he shared his secret spit-shine technique with me.

But when he drank, Harold became a fighter. Up close, you could see the evidence in several neck and facial scars. Women drifted into his life, and then, as his weakness for drink began to manifest itself, they drifted out again.

During the summers when I worked for my father, I often saw Harold climbing up and down the extension ladders. On Monday mornings, his body would respond to the abuse he'd inflicted on it during the week-end bender, and he would wrap his arms around the ladder and slide to the ground, screaming in pain, retching and rolling to relieve the cramps.

My father tolerated such behavior up to a point, but was also poised to terminate Harold's stint of employment should things get too far out of hand.

One night, Dad hired Harold to paint the inside floors of a meat-packing plant, after-hours and unsupervised. He was to apply anti-slipping silica products so the freshly-painted floors would grip well enough to prevent falls.

The plant's security guard called later to say that a drunken workman was splashing paint on the walls, ceilings, floors—everything in sight. This was an expensive disaster for my dad, and Harold again lost his job.

When my father died several years ago, our whole family gathered in the old Sioux City funeral home for his wake. We were solemnly seated in front of his open casket when, about half-way through the service, the funeral director tapped my brother on the shoulder. "There's an urgent phone call for you in my office," he whispered.

My brother followed him out of the room, and returned a few minutes later with a smile, "It was Harold. He wants to pay his respects, but he's just too drunk to show up."

That call became the benediction for my father's life, underscoring his grateful dedication to Alcoholics Anonymous, his humble tolerance for each man's frailties, and his total forgiveness.

During his drinking years, my father had inflicted a good deal of pain on the people he loved. Afterwards, he was more willing to forgive others than to forgive himself.

Thanks, Dad. May you rest in peace.

# My Dentist's Hands

During Sunday services, I stand up, head bowed, eyes closed for the Lord's Prayer, extending my hand to the elderly stranger next to me. His calloused hand grasps mine and I'm struck with a keen longing for my father, whose strong fingers held mine in the same firm grip.

This somatic memory of my father's hand resonates around this simple grasp. I sense his ghostly presence with a love I haven't known for years.

Tears slide down my face. A feeling of love and joy for my father permeates me with a warm sense of grace. God has given me this unexpected, intimate moment, allowed me to touch my father one more time. I am grateful for this surreal reunion and hope the prayer will never end.

At last I open my eyes to look at the man next to me. He is not my dad, but I sense the same towering tree of life. The man turns, gives me a nod, a squeeze of my hand and a small smirk. I am self-conscious of my dentist's hands, soft from frequent washings, latex gloves, a lack of manual labor.

To solve life's problems my father relied on brute strength. His arms were as thick as large oak logs.

My father dreamed of the highly educated, healing hands of a veterinarian, but those dreams were slapped down by the throes of the Great Depression.

He sacrificed personal goals for the urgent needs of his mother and younger siblings, plagued by the unshakeable curse of the Great Depression, alcoholism, job losses, floods, failed enterprises and other struggles.

He loved the soil. I cannot remember a time when my parents didn't have dirt under their nails. Their Dakota homesteaders' roots grew deep into their being, so they were constantly digging, tilling, planting, hoeing and harvesting in tune with the earth.

I stare at my hands as if I'd never seen them before—the scar on my left thumb where I sliced my knuckle cleaning fish at our Saskatchewan cabin; the misshapen nails on my right hand where a little league baseball broke off four fingernails. My hands are tanned, soft, wrinkled, creased, asymmetrical, scarred, crossed with raised exposed veins. They appear to be foreign. I continue to examine them, hoping to find similar parental genetic traits, but my hands have not earned their history. The only features I share with my father are the sun freckles reflecting our passion for the outdoors.

Suddenly I realize that my father's labor has given me these hands, the clean nails, the small, short fingers skilled to perform the delicate procedures that allow me to heal, to be an extension of God's work.

I am looking at the hands my parents wanted me to have.

# Facing Mortality

## Good Friday

It was an overcast day, and the dark clouds, brimming with sorrow and ominous dread, seemed to match my inner state. My rich Catholic guilt, ingrained in me by the dutiful and ever-so-holy Franciscan Sisters during my childhood years, was at work in the depths of my gut as a re-occurring ulcerating lesion of spiritual inadequacies and personal failings.

Repent and live to the highest!

On that Good Friday, I spent several hours face-to-face with the frailties of human life as my old college roommate and life-long friend Joe shared with me the agonized rants and reflections of a dying man. Joe had been diagnosed with a brain tumor called "astrocytoma" from which scant few survive. I had been granted a seat on the emotional roller-coaster of his final days, and was honored to share a part of that difficult journey.

That day started as we reminisced over our morning coffee about the carefree exploits of our college days, and our shared determination to attain the highest levels of academic success in the midst of the inescapable temptations of college social life. We both indulged in alcohol, music, and party-hearty relations with coeds, and pursued seemingly random paths of intellectual discovery, during our college years, but rarely did we allow those distractions to undermine our sense of focus. As a result, we both met our youthful goals and pursued the professions we'd set our sights on.

Joe and I lost touch for quite some time, but re-connected. Catching up with the many lost years, we rekindled our friendship by swapping stories that reaffirmed the values we continued to share in a spirit of spontaneity and celebration.

The talk took on a darker tone as Joe began to describe his final day at the office: He decided to continue his optometry practice as long as he felt capable, knowing that the tumor would eventually win out.

"One cold January day," he told me, "I drove to work as I had for more than twenty years and began a typical morning. After I had completed a few eye examinations, I was startled to find something subtle had changed in my motor skills. It hit me hard to realize that my health had finally deteriorated to the point where I could no longer work. All the years of education and career challenges suddenly stopped; it was time for me to go.

"Without notifying my staff, I found a small cardboard box in which to pack up my belongings. I walked around from room to room searching for the treasures of my life, gathering all the personal items that I wanted to take home. But now the common things that I had used daily took on a new and different value. I was amazed at the simple mementos I had collected. My daughter's watercolor painting, a hand-carved sailboat that a long-time patient had given me, family photos that had kept me focused on tough days, a pen holder from my wife, and many small trinkets that reminded me of people and places of my past. Not one item in the box had anything to do with my career; everything had to do with the people I loved.

"I walked to the front desk where my staff was standing by and quietly announced, 'I'm done.' Then I limped to the door, clutching my precious box, and left work for the last time."

As we talked I could see Joe's stamina wane, and when extreme lethargy finally set in, he excused himself for a nap. The neural deterioration, drugs, and altered sleep patterns had shortened Joe's energy fuse. While he rested, Joe's wife and I took the opportunity to talk intimately about Joe's condition.

I asked her about her perception of how Joe was handling things? Was there anything I could do? How could I be of service, today or in the future, even across the distance of 300 miles that usually separated us?

After skirting around the issue for a while, Lila finally got to the unspoken taboo in Joe's mind: Death. Joe was fighting hard to beat this tumor, and felt that even the slightest reference to the concept of death would send him down the slippery slope of moral weakness, self-doubt, failure, and a self-fulfilling diagnosis of doom. He was not going to go that route. He was not going to fail. He had been flying around the country, attempting to find the experimental treatment, the magic bullet that would insure his survival. Unfortunately the cost of such treatments was staggering, while their effectiveness was nil. This not-so-slow hemorrhaging of their dwindling financial resources, combined with Joe's refusal to make even the sketchiest and most speculative plans for his family's future, had brought yet one more element of distress into an already-miserable situation.

Lila hoped that I would be able to introduce the subject of death, funerals and estate planning into the afternoon's discussion.

Having practiced dentistry in a hospital setting for twenty-five years, I was intimately familiar with the world of disease and death, and had developed a comfortable acceptance of end-of-life issues as well as a certain degree of frankness when discussing them. Sometimes we have a choice in life either to laugh or cry. I prefer to laugh, and I was hoping that Joe, too, would appreciate that approach.

After Joe had finished his nap we ate lunch, accompanied by ice-cold beer that seemed to rekindle the mood of our college days.

With renewed strength Joe filled me in on the circumstances of his insurance company, which had denied him disability. Even though the Social Security Administration had already determined that Joe was eligible under their standards, his private policy would not recognize his obvious disability, regardless of his growing and dis-figurative tumor, his swollen tissues (due to large doses of cortisone) and his severely altered gait, which caused him to drag his droopy leg.

Lila and I attempted to exchange small talk as Joe endured yet another frustrating inquiry with his insurance agent, followed by an equally unproductive phone call to the mortgage company handling his refinancing request. As I sat there listening quietly, I found it difficult to suppress a rising rage at the callous insensitivity and niggardly bureaucratic stonewalling being offered to a man suffering with the final stages of a terminal brain tumor!

After this second dead-end telephone conversation Joe crashed into the over-stuffed couch with a sigh of, "Oh, shit," and said, "Want another beer?"

"Sure, why not."

As we decompressed I started into my role as a storyteller, delicately broaching the subjects of death and funerals. A few years previously my mother and sister had passed away within a month of each other, and I was able to personalize the story by describing how starkly different their responses to death had been.

My mother somehow knew she was going to die soon, so on Easter Sunday, 2000, nine days before her death, she had cleared her slate with me. She stood in the doorway that afternoon, tilting her head to visualize my presence through a murky cloud of macular degeneration. An ocular stroke in her left eye and the ravages of eighty-three years had left her legally blind.

Her face showed the simple life she had desired and lived. Deep wrinkles and random age spots were tattooed badges of survival. Her graying brown hair had become slightly whiter around the edges since the last time I was home. She still curled it with pink sponges in her ever-simple way.

My mother was never glamorous, always uncomplicated. Her dress, which almost resembled a plain, life-long uniform, was light blue and covered with a pattern of small flowers. There were also a few food stains on the front, undetected by her ailing eyes.

My family was already loading the car, and as I subtly tried to pull away, I could not let go of my angry disappointment that she had not taken the opportunity to move into a nearby senior housing unit when her name had finally reached the top of the list. Despite her life-long desire to live in a new place, she denied herself the luxury, perhaps out of fear. The threadbare linoleum in the narrow hall reflected her choice to remain within her own familiarity.

A couple of years earlier when Mom had suffered the stroke, she attempted to lay guilt on me by hinting that she should consider a nursing home. I suggested that all she needed was a roommate—someone with healthy eyes.

She assumed I meant the company of a man and shook her head, "I'm afraid I'd get a talker." My dad had the Irish gift of gab and when he went into assisted living, she may have enjoyed the peace of being alone.

Torn between my waiting family and my aged mother, I blurted out, "I've got to go."

But Mom pulled me back into her musty apartment, frugally chilly and curtained off from the sunlight outside, to say her private good-bye. Her family were stoic Norwegians, so a nod and a wink would always do for a hug.

"I tried to do my best," she said. "There were a couple of things that I didn't like about myself. I was a jealous person, and I wish I'd known better how to show my love."

Then she hugged me hard, a hug that's lasted forever.

A week later, on a Monday night, she died in the hall on her way to bed.

Looking back at our final moments, I understand the meaning of perfect parenting. I've never felt the need to be jealous and although I express my love daily, it's never enough.

No regrets."

When she died I had an overwhelming feeling of peace and resolve. There were no regrets of not addressing those remaining unspoken words. I told Joe that my mother's last words were truly a gift and that he had the rare opportunity to clear the slate with all of his family members. If he did so, I said, they would be forever grateful as I was.

I continued my story by mentioning that during my mother's funeral, my sister knew that she would soon die, so during the days surrounding my mother's funeral she shared her many wishes for her own internment. Betty had her issues with organized religion, and what she considered the "voodoo ceremonies" of the Catholic Church were not important to her. Her love of the river would be her final statement. She requested that we dump her ashes in the Missouri River while Tina Turner's "Rolling on the River" blasted from a boom box. We did as she wished and whole family celebrated her dumping with smiles, laughter, and laying red roses in the water along with her floating ashes as the massive muddy river peacefully dispersed her mortal remains.

The River was her place. Surprisingly, the notion of her ashes being redistributed and recycled throughout the globe by the waterways of our Mother Earth still touches me from time to time. In my day-to-day life, out of the blue, the sight of a body of water can elicit a smile and a wonderful memory of my sister Betty.

We all are only seconds away from our own death, so we need to keep the conversation open. Live a life that you want to live. None of us get out of this world alive.

I also shared with Joe a few of my experiences with many hospice patients, including the one who was kicked out and went on to live a long full life.

That memorable day of living life fully with my dearest friends eventually had to end. As I was leaving to head back to my in-laws for the remaining Easter weekend, Joe said: "Pat, you are going to live a long life."

The statement caught me off guard: Joe had never previously shown any gift for prophecy. "You don't know that," I replied.

He cocked his head with renewed energy and responded, "Yes I do. You will live a long life." This time the powerful confidence in his words was even more perplexing.

"How in the hell would you know that?" I said.

There was a long pause and the silence was screaming for an end, then he returned "Because you already have!"

After that weekend we exchanged many phone calls, invariably in the early morning, since Joe's disrupted sleep patterns left him awake at that time and I was alone in the office at 6:00 AM. During the last of them, in November 2003, we freely expressed our love in a way that men seldom do, and Joe described the difficulty his own father had conveying such emotions. At those times Joe would sometimes taunt his father by saying, "Dad, can't you feel the love in the room?"

Back at my in-law's house, my wife's ninety-seven-year-old grandmother, shared with me at Easter that she was not going to Heaven. I immediately responded "Oh, a nice lady like you will surely go to Heaven." She quickly returned "If He wanted me He would have taken me a long time ago."

# You Did a Good Job

*The heart pumps the body's supply of blood approx. 5 quarts (4.7 liters) in an average adult.*

– New Book of Popular Science

A distinguished elderly lady waltzed into my dental office one day in need of a minor denture adjustment. A few minutes later I was the prime suspect in a murder investigation.

"Margaret" had been escorted to my fifth-floor office from a transitional rehabilitation center. She was a tall, thin lady in her early seventies, with curly gray hair, wearing makeup and street clothes. She was an "in-patient."

She couldn't speak because of a hole in her throat, a surgical tracheotomy required to remove a cancerous voice box. Her chart showed she'd had multiple surgeries and several courses of radiation in the neck region, but otherwise she appeared to be in good health.

Margaret pulled out a tablet and wrote, "I have a sore spot under my denture," pointing inside her mouth. I removed her upper plate, smeared it with PIP paste to identify the pressure spots, made a quick adjustment and fitted it back inside.

She smiled with relief, "You did a good job."

Margaret then returned to the reception area, and while my office manager Betty called for her escort, she headed off toward the public restroom down the hall.

I was checking another patient when Betty rushed in, "Doctor Foy, I need you in the waiting area now!"

Margaret was sitting in a chair, gazing into space, blood spouting from the hole in her neck with every heartbeat.

"Call 911!" I shouted.

My first instinct was to stop the bleeding. I placed my bare thumb inside the large stoma and moved it around the warm, slimy tissue, searching for the magic spot to compress the carotid artery. But the blood kept drenching my hand. I realized almost immediately this wasn't a case for the Boy Scouts. I was out of my league.

I raced across the hall and returned with a young family physician in tow. He assessed her condition at a glance and asked, "What's her name?"

"Margaret."

He looked her right in the eyes and said softly, "Margaret, we're going to lose you."

I was stunned. It seemed unbelievable there was nothing we could do save her life. She was still upright in the chair, with the blood pulsing out more slowly as the volume decreased. I felt helpless, but needed to take some action. "Should we get her down on the floor?" The doctor nodded. We each took a side, and with Betty supporting her head, we lowered her gently to the rug.

All at once the blood began gushing into her mouth and nose, running into her eyes, pooling in red, sticky liquid on the floor. All the blood that had drained into her lungs was pouring out and the volume was astounding, unimaginable. My hands and knees were covered, Betty's hands and arms were drenched, and she began to sob.

The doctor kneeling beside Margaret kept checking her pulse and before long it had faded away entirely.

A few minutes later a barrage of rescue people began to arrive. First a gang of firemen lugging black cases raced through the door and stopped cold, their faces sagging in disbelief. The EMTs from the ambulance company were immediately stood down by the firemen. The hospital attendants joined them, and the congregation that had assembled in our office began to ooze out into the hall.

Suddenly a policeman shoved through the crowd, took a brief look around at the supine body and all the blood, and shouted, "Don't touch anything. I'm calling in homicide!"

My mind started spinning out of control. I'd never felt so frightened and deflated in my life. A gruesome, bloody death had just occurred in my office. My scrubs were soaked at the knees, my hands were smeared with blood, and we were in the hands of an authority with the IQ of room temperature.

My startled dental assistant and hygienist came out and were sternly instructed, "Do not talk to each other!. I am going to put each of you in a different room."

Where was this going? Would I be accused of murdering a patient? Would I be arrested and taken off to jail? Dental school, a hospital-based residency and twenty years of experience had not prepared me for this. I felt so at a loss that my natural instincts to resist or fight back abandoned me entirely. I was ready to be cuffed and hauled away. The mental trauma and that helpless deflation are hauntingly memorable even today.

As the officer started my interrogation, the homicide squad arrived to photograph the scene. Margaret's body still lay in her blood on the waiting room floor.

The young physician who had shared the woman's dying moments alongside me suddenly called from my cramped personal office. "Doctor Foy, the medical examiner wants to talk to you!" The commando cop nodded his approval and I went to the phone.

The medical examiner immediately absolved me of any guilt. There was nothing we could have done to save Margaret's life. Cancer patients normally die in this way. A tumor erodes through a major vessel and the person bleeds to death internally. Nancy's death was more visibly horrific than most, what with the blood spouting out her surgical site, but not unusual considering the circumstances of her health.

The examiner asked to speak with the police officer, and I felt an uplifting rush of freedom as I walked down the hall to get him. After a short time the officer returned from my office and angrily announced that the case was out of his hands, and unceremoniously left the building.

I went to check on my staff and to assure them that everything was okay. I'd asked one of the hospital nurses to help us deal with the mental anguish this crisis might cause. She provided handouts and advised us not to internalize the experience. She recommended that we call in a colleague who could relate professionally. We should also tell our families and ask them to report any behavior or mood changes.

As we put together the pieces later a clearer picture emerged of what precisely had happened. While she was waiting for her escort, Margaret had used the ladies room.  A slight straining apparently caused enough pressure to break the carotid artery. Dark red blood had splashed on the bright lemon walls of the restroom; we could follow the trail down the hall to our office, where the front of the desk was also spattered. A pattern of blood across the floor of the waiting room marked the path of several distraught laps Margaret took before settling into the chair.

Her body was finally moved to the hospital morgue, and we were left with the blood. The office building's crew, inexperienced in removing blood stains, tried to clean the hall carpet with bleach. Permanent spots still remind us of a day we'd prefer to forget.

We cancelled all the remaining scheduled appointments for the day, and there was nothing left for me to do but lock up and go home. I was locking the back door when a patient showed up holding a porcelain crown in his hand. His appearance was a gift. This simple act of normal dental care was a perfect way to end my work day.

At home, I gave my wife the hand-out and told her I needed to go for a walk. It had snowed recently, and the new coating of pristine white fluff filled the outdoors with a tranquil winter beauty. After a couple of hours of kicking through the white powder, I finally started to make peace with my day.

In an effort to be helpful, my wife had begun to do a few of my household chores, but I felt the need to grab a hold of some normal routines. That night our two young daughters were scheduled for skating lessons and I volunteered to take them.

I was sitting in the stands when a local fireman came over asking, "How was your day?" I knew at once he'd heard about the event from his wife, who was a medical secretary in our building. He shared a few horror stories of his own and reassured me that facing death is difficult, even for a trained professional. I was grateful for the thoughtful gesture.

The next morning our staff rallied with a renewed sense of spirit, and the medical community offered surprising support. As a token of understanding and compassion, a hospital administrator offered to help cover the cost of the carpet replacement.

As the only dentist on our medical campus, I'd often felt myself to be a bit of an outsider, regarded by my colleagues in the building as different from a "real doctor." Now that I'd held mortality in my hands, and watched life slip away in truly gruesome fashion, they responded as if I'd now been initiation into their club.

That day was the beginning of new understanding about how fragile and merciful life can be. We can't control all of the events in our lives, but we can adjust our responses, and be attentive to the network of personal affections that keep us afloat when we seem to have lost our buoyancy.

Margaret's final words, delivered a few minutes before she met her end, on a subject as minor as the fitting of a denture, became a benediction, "You did a good job."

# A Class I Missed in Dental School?

Immersed in my private practice of dentistry for 25 years, I considered myself fortunate; things were rolling along quite smoothly. Until Jesse came into our practice. Jesse was a very serene, soft-spoken, tall, sleek, ravishing young black woman in her early thirties. Her unassertive manner and gracious attitude always made her visits pleasant and delightful. She had perfect dental health with absolutely no sign of any other health concerns. Her only dental concern was that she had slightly narrow central incisors resulting in a diastema (space) between her front two teeth. The small space in her teeth represented the only flaw in her otherwise goddess-like physical appearance.

Over the years, I have learned that such small defects can sear into the psyche of a person relentlessly. No matter how insignificant the problem may actually be, it looms out of all proportion and mercilessly undermines a person's self-perception. Jesse's dream was to have that diastema corrected with dental veneers. She was the one driving her own treatment plan. Her radiant beauty was not affected one iota by her teeth, but it was a mental gremlin to her self-esteem.

After long discussions and reviewing all of her options, I finally caved in to her request to veneer her front two teeth. The case was one hundred and ten percent successful, and she broadcast her beauty and her confidence instantaneously. I had made her day.

Months went by. Jesse was scheduled for a routine cleaning visit but failed to show up for the appointment. That was out of character for her. We called and left a message on her answering machine regarding the missed appointment. A day later her mother called to inform our receptionist that Jesse would not be coming back. She had died of complications from a bleeding gastric ulcer.

Young, healthy, seductive enchanters are not supposed to die. *They never told me in dental school that my patients were going to die.*

At first I was numbed by the news of Jesse's death. Then, when it dawned on me that perhaps hundreds of my patients would die before I turned off my overhead lamp for the last time, I got angry. I felt betrayed. The relationships I enjoy with the people I work with and treat make going to work very gratifying. I feel honored to be part of their lives and feel extremely close to many of them. Though I had experienced patients dying before, Jesse was the unexpected slap in the face that made me appreciate the harsh reality of the experience.

I was unable to shake the shock of her death. It haunted me and forced me to review my previous experiences with patients who died, or who were grieving for others. On several occasions, I had witnessed the pain caused by a loved one dying play itself out in my dental chair, and the variety of emotions expressed had been enlightening. There are no rules or established norms for grieving. Over time, listening to my patients vent, mourn, laugh, cry, celebrate, and in other ways share their personal feelings has given me an education that very few are privileged to receive.

Looking back at such moments, it occurred to me that early in my career I was not terribly adept at finding the correct words for a grieving family. When I purchased my practice, I inherited a family from the previous dentist which included three teenagers. Their mother was going through chemotherapy for breast cancer. I saw her only once before she died, and stymied by ignorance and inexperience, I fumbled for words of sympathy the next time I treated her children.

In time I found it less difficult to find the proper words, and even developed a healthy curiosity around how families differ in their process of letting loved ones pass. I watched my own family and my wife's family react in completely different ways. I began to re-examine my own experience with death. I relived my childhood experiences with the death of grandparents and pets. I recounted how relatives, parents, and siblings processed the experience of grieving. Knowing that each family and each person develops his or her own "culture" in this area helped me to accept my own helpless ignorance.

I cannot pretend to know what each person honestly needs or wants at this hard time in life, but acknowledging their loved one is a great start. Also, expressing your thoughts, memories, and sympathy is always appropriate and welcomed by the grieving. Offer your willingness to listen or offer to help in any way possible. This is the least you can do for people you have shared a relationship with over the years.

Shortly after the shock of Jesse's death had subsided, another of my patients, Jane, came in for a minor dental repair. Jane had lost her sixteen-year-old son in a motor vehicle accident years before. He had been a happy, slightly rebellious, robust, energetic teenager with a great smile and a boyish sense of humor. We had not spoken of Christian for years, but during one Christmas season, cognizant that the holidays often stimulate many memories of the past for a parent, I asked Jane, "How old would Christian be today?"

She lifted her chin and smiled. Her eyes focused on my eyes. There was a peaceful glow that emanated from her face. With joy and gratitude in the tone of her voice, she shared, "Christian would be thirty-five. We really had a lot of fun together. I loved him so much."

There was pure exuberance and celebration in those words. Clearly she welcomed the opportunity to shared with me a bit of her life with her son. Such moments were perhaps not common.

All of us hope that to be remembered after we leave this earth. The families on my dad's side immediately start celebrating the life of the deceased after the tears vanish. We laugh and share fond memories, rehashing the events that have touched our lives. I remember many funerals where laughter was so prominent that it was hard to imagine sorrow was present.

In the process of exploring these often-taboo areas of death and grieving, I realized we dentists experience loss in other ways as well. When patients and families leave our practices for one reason or another, it still feels like a loss and elicits an emotional response, though the emotions that surface are in each case unique. We may feel anger, betrayal, loneliness, depression, or rejection. It's important that we acknowledge those feelings for the benefit of our long-term mental health. Grieving should be addressed as part of our education, though the subject has never been formally broached in my entire career.

Many dentists complain that we need more business classes in order to run a dental practice successfully. I contend the lack of emotional education may produce a more harmful result.

# Last Words

*Whatever words we utter should be chosen with care, for people will hear them and be influenced by them for good and evil.*

– Buddha

As a twenty-five-year-old dental resident in Minneapolis, MN, I was involved as a nurse anesthesiologist at a Veterans Administration Hospital in a General Practice Residency Program in Dentistry. It was a teaching hospital, so it was not unusual for a resident to serve in this capacity.

Along with learning about the affects of general anesthesia drugs, how to maintain an airway and how to continue respirations after the muscles of breathing had been paralyzed, I also discovered how people reveal themselves with their last words as I pushed in the IV drugs.

Each person had a distinctive reaction to the drugs, which induced a lack of inhibitions. Some seemed perfectly clear-headed; others slurred their words and were incapable of lucid thought. A few let out piercing cries of desperation as they face the possibility of imminent death. The conversations with these patients was never routine.

Kenny, one of our youngest patients, was from a poor family in a remote part of Wisconsin who had joined the U. S. Army at seventeen. His cleft lip had been repaired as a child, but because his hard palate was never corrected, his speech had a nasal tone and he lacked the teeth and bone for a normal smile. All this had undoubtedly scarred his self-esteem. Now that he had completed his four years of service, the Veterans Administration was going to correct his cleft palate and fix his teeth.

Intoxicated with his anticipation of a new life, he announced "Look out, ladies! Here comes a new Kenny!"

A middle-aged man who was suffering from a possible internal intestinal bleed came to the operating room weak and groggy, but he was smiling. Knowing that his prognosis was tenuous, I found the expression puzzling.

We positioned him on the operating table, prepared the IV, and he graciously thanked us. Then he looked to the upper corner of the operating room and said, "Lord, I am ready. Take my hand and lead me where you may."

The drugs were pushed, his eyes closed and the routine of opening his gut got underway. When the snarls of brownish, snake-like intestines were exposed, we knew we were in for a desperate ride.

The man's blood pressure dropped quickly and we instantly tapped bags of blood to transfuse. The cold blood was warmed as it passed through a line heater before entering his arm. Suddenly his blood pressure dropped again, precipitously.

I squeezed the bags of blood with all my strength to force in as much as possible. Desperately we tried to maintain his vitality.

The time of death was 10:08 A.M. The mood changed from frantic to a sullen sense of defeat. I was haunted by his sudden, helpless end, yet comforted by his last words.

My youthful curiosity was piqued by the various ways that people coped when faced with a very real possibility of death, and each day I looked forward to new insights. It seemed as if I were watching an intimate dance of human existence. At various stages of my own subsequent development, one or another of those death-bed remarks has returned to me with renewed significance.

*Tell my family that I love them … I hope the gates are open … I am so sorry that I never knew my kid … Why did I waste my life? … Bless me father for I have sinned … Is this all there is? … I realize now that my parents sacrificed everything for me … God is here … It's over … I was so in love with my wife … I never got a chance to say good bye … I should have listened to my Sergeant … Why was I put on earth? … I honestly tried my best.*

What will be your last words? What will be mine?

# Lessons from a Dead Dentist

*Quality is never an accident; it is always the result of high intention, sincere effort, intelligent direction and skillful execution; it represents the wise choice of many alternatives.*

– William A. Foster (1917-1945)
U. S. Marines, Medal of Honor, KIA Okinawa

The unforgiving reality of dentistry is that the quality of our work usually remains in a patient's mouth. Every six months, our triumphs, challenges and failures return for inspection and stand as a permanent record of our clinical skills. No human being can fill every single tooth perfectly, so once in a while, when the filling or crown didn't turn out as planned, we must be allowed to take a "Mulligan."

My first dental associate position was in the early eighties when the standard of care consisted mainly of amalgams (silver fillings), some crowns, and a few bridges. My boss had bought the practice from the estate of a dentist who had shot his wife, two kids and the dog before turning the gun on himself. This professional legacy continued to haunt us.

The office manager/receptionist who had worked for the dentist stayed on. She was a master of the appointment book and took pride in scheduling a productive day. On the night before his suicide, the dentist had taken home his appointment book, so the next day she couldn't cancel the patients' scheduled times. Every hour she faced someone who'd made the unnecessary trip with news of his death. Consequently, when she went home at night, she hid the appointment book.

My curious spirit drove me to seek out some insightful answers to this dentist's demise. Why would anyone do such a thing? Radiographs and oral exams had me peering into the mouths of his former patients, hoping for direction to my answer. The revealing evidence left behind was the quality of his dentistry over the years.

It appeared as if the man had simply failed to admit his imperfections. It is not unusual for a dentist to place several thousand restorations (fillings) during a calendar year. During that time perhaps twenty restorations or more might require additional attention. If he failed to re-do the work as the needs came to light, the numbers would eventually add up over a decade of practice. And they did.

Perhaps one day, in a state of depression, he had witnessed, by sheer coincident, and unending parade of inferior work, and knew that his name was on it. He arrived at the conclusion that the world would be better off without him.

Most procedures allow us to take another shot at our work. When we start out in our careers, the re-dos and re-makes severely affect our financial bottom-line; but in time, we do better work, and retain a degree of pride in having maintained a high standard of care. Our patients appreciate our willingness to honor their complaints and re-do the things that just don't sit or feel right.

Examining my predecessor's records, and pondering his fate, convinced me of the importance of rectifying unacceptable work as soon as possible. To this day, that harsh lesson allows me to accept my imperfections as a normal fact of life, take a Mulligan from time to time, and to sleep easy with myself as a result.

"You're not happy with that? Let's try it again."

# Grace

Raging anger, blame and confusion. Those were the emotions I experienced whenever I was notified of a death of a loved one or a friend. I have reacted that way my whole life, but never understood why.

Someone recently asked me to recall my first memory, and it was the death of our cocker spaniel, Skippy. I was four years old and too young to understand the permanence of death or even what had happened. But I had observed and learned from the various reactions of our family.

Skippy had been a constant companion to my two teenage sisters, and their crying seemed endless. My mother and nine-year-old brother were also shedding tears, but in a sad, silent, reserved manner.

My father's reaction was completely different. He shed no tears. He was steaming mad but I did not remember why. As the rest of my family wept, my father paced the floor ranting with anger. He was projecting strength, and that behavior became imprinted in my own response to grief.

How we grieve is a learned behavior. There is not a right or wrong way to grieve. There are no time limits. Tradition and cultures affect how our families process loss. Each person learns from a lifetime of experiences.

This is why I feel blessed to have met Dee and her daughter, Grace.

"I broke out an old filling, Doctor," Dee said to me one day. "Can you tell me how old that filling was?"

This seemingly normal conversation in a dental office was the overture to a life-changing experience.

Dee had been a patient since 1975, even before I joined the practice in 1981.

"I can find out by looking in your chart."

As I was digging through her file, removing all the colored sheets of paper, I came across the poster she had made for our staff eight years earlier after the death of her ten-year-old daughter.

Her mother had brought Grace into our office back in the 1980s for routine dental care. Grace was mentally delayed with involuntary hand movements from Rett Syndrome, an inherited childhood neurological and developmental disorder believed to be caused by a genetic mutation. She had difficulty cooperating as a dental patient, but her mother discovered that bringing a boom-box with some of Grace's favorite tunes would relax her. We would shut the door to the operatory, and with Mom's boom-box blasting, an assistant and I performed all the dental care necessary.

After awhile the routine seemed easy and became part of Grace's normal care in our chair. The music was loud, but the feeling of accomplishment was louder. We were able to provide Grace with the simple dentistry she required.

I do not remember the details of Grace's death, but I believe it was an accident at her day-care center.

The poster in Dee's chart was filled on both sides with quotes, clippings and pictures from Grace's classmates pasted on yellow construction paper about 20 by 30 inches. There was a picture of Grace in the midst of three of her friends, who were holding hands and gently supporting her so she could stand. The picture had a title in bold print: "NO MAN IS AN ISLAND," and underneath in smaller print, "Bridges are being built to our severely disabled citizens."

Down in the corner was a color picture of Grace smiling sweetly and a note she had dictated to her mother expressing her appreciation for the loving care our office provided. "Thank you for helping me in my life and for comforting my family in my death. Remember what I have taught you. I love you. Good Bye. Grace."

At the moment, I did not know what to do with the poster. Should I leave it in the chart and continuing looking for the entry regarding the broken filling? I was hesitant to pull it out and upset a grieving mother, but I took the risk.

To my amazement Dee lit up like the sun. With love and joy in her voice, she uttered these astonishing words:

"God gave me ten years with that angel!"

I was left speechless.

As I repaired her broken tooth, Dee's words resonated in my mind. Wow! How could she have such faith in God? How could she come to a point to be thankful for Grace and not be devastated by the loss of her daughter?

The radiance of Dee's pure love reached deep into my soul, grabbed my being and forever affected my outlook towards God, love, and parenting.

That night as I drove home, I thought of my two daughters and what they meant to me. Sarah was five and my Katherine was two years old. They were young and innocent. Life to them was an uncomplicated process of learning something new each day. The notion of death was not yet a part of their experience—not even a pet, much less a relative. I remember my oldest once told me that she had a previous life, but I don't know where that came from or if it is a natural human fantasy.

I mentally projected the possibility of losing one of my girls and asked myself whether I could deal with such devastation emotionally. What state of mind do you need to get there? How do I parent today so I have no regrets if we experience a loss? Could I be faithful enough to feel blessed and grateful for only having a short time with them? If I did lose a daughter, would I be grieving merely my own expectations for them? What is our role on this earth? Does a small child understand her legacy? Is death with peace only for the chronically ill? Is happiness for our children the ultimate in a parent's sense of fulfillment?

I had a restless night, haunted with doubt and uncertainty. The trial of God's purpose and goal continued to wrestle in my head. I finally came to accept mortality. I asked God for His help and insight through prayer and meditation. Faithfully, I was left with small realizations—to enjoy and appreciate the moments we have been given, and to forgive myself for not always being the perfect father.

My children have given me a new set of eyes in this world. A child's life allows us not only to nurture them, but also to nurture ourselves and taste our youth again. I want to be there for them, so I'd take better care of myself. A child demands our time and support, but if done right we share and are graced with mutual love.

My parents were taken for granted for years, until I became a parent. When my father passed away, I knew he had left a huge legacy that lives in me and is appreciated and valued. My father knew how to play and he was not afraid of work. He conveyed that strong work ethic with a twist of joy to me. This gift makes my daily interaction with patients a pleasure and I love to share their lives with mine.

We all cherish the values our parents instilled in us and hope to pass them on to our children. There are also struggles within ourselves that we're far less eager to perpetuate.

I asked my sister to enlighten me about the details of Skippy's death. She said the cocker spaniel had been tied up outside the grocery store and began barking for my sisters to return. An animal protection officer overreacted and tried to quiet Skippy with a tranquilizer gun. The shot was fatal.

My father's angry reaction was directed at the rogue officer who had inflicted senseless suffering onto our family. To a four-year-old, he was the man of strength and wisdom whose behavior I should emulate.

The uplifting lesson from Dee and Grace was a daily celebration of living in the moment. Grace's legacy was to teach me the faith of her mother and appreciation of my daily experiences with my own children; to plan a good future, but also to respond positively when life throws a curve.

That may be a hard lesson to adopt, but I must say it helped when I lost both my sister and my mother within a month. I experienced a feeling of loss of those family members with that old anger, but I was quickly celebrating the things that they brought to the table of life. Our family first dealt with the details of the funerals, then we laughed, loved, shared moments, and both were put to rest with peace

Grief is such an individual expression of loss, each of us needs to navigate our emotions to the point where that peace can be achieved.

"God gave me ten years of that angel!"

# Eosophilic Myalgia

*We cannot seek or attain health, wealth, learning, justice or kindness in general. Action is always specific, concrete, individualized, unique.*

– Benjamin Jowett

I will never take a pill ever again." That was the blunt comment delivered to me by the station nurse who had been assigned that day as Emily's charge nurse.

I had just arrived at Abbot-Northwestern for a dental consultation. The comment surprised me, coming from the mouth of a veteran nurse who had witnessed the healing effects of many pharmaceuticals over a long career.

Emily was a thirty-year-old attorney, very petite but now also very frail as a result of having self-prescribed an over-the-counter health food supplement for her sleeping problems. The product's active ingredient, "L-tryptophan" is same one found in turkey meat, which makes you doze off in front of the television set after the Thanksgiving Day dinner. It was once also widely administered as an appetite suppressor.

Emily's doctor's surmised that a bad batch of L-tryptophan had inflicted her with a disorder called "eosophilic myalgia," which stimulates the red blood cells to viciously attack and destroy muscle cells. The affliction came to the awareness of the medical community only during the 1980's when the supplement containing L-tryptophan was being mass-produced in Japan. Because the rate, severity, length, and location of the attacks varied from patient to patient, the disorder remained little-understood and was difficult to diagnose, though delay in treatment could lead to tragic outcomes.

The first time I visited Emily was soon after the onset of the eosophilic myalgia when she had just been admitted to the hospital. Her initial dental problem was that of a crown that had come loose for unknown reasons. During the brief time I spent with Emily, she seemed buried in self-pity and confusion, and I imagined that our professional relationship would be brief. I was wrong.

A few weeks later I was called again to the hospital to see Emily, this time for broken teeth. When I walked into her room I was shocked by the look of her ashen, death-like, sullen, trembling face and quivering lower mandible. The attack of the red cells had aggressively wasted away at her muscle tissue to the point where even simple body movements were difficult, and her jaw muscles were now so weak that they were no longer able to counteract the weight of her jaw without a weak uncontrollable tremor.

Her mouth hung opened and the enamel on her teeth, deprived of normal lubrication from saliva, had grown dry and begun to fracture and chip. The only treatment available to me at that time was to smooth the rough surfaces in hope of avoiding irritation to the tongue. It seemed like a pathetically anemic response to her deteriorating overall health but it was all I could do.

A few months later I was called in to see Emily again. I could see that things had finally begun to changed for the better, and Emily's attitude had also improved. She developed an attitude of a fighter, even though she had lost her ability to breathe on her own and was now hooked up to a mechanical ventilator. Her tongue muscles had also came back allowing her to swallow and speak. However, her facial muscles and her jaw muscles were still too weak to function normally, and this created some new problems. The strength of the tongue's muscles, meeting no counteractive forces from her facial muscles, was pushing her upper and lower teeth outward, thus expanding her dental arches and creating gaps between her teeth. I had been called in to do something to stop the movement.

We eventually constructed upper and lower Hawley retainers which we hoped would counteract the spreading forces of the muscular tongue. The retainers worked to Emily's satisfaction, but her health insurance company balked at the idea of paying for an orthodontic appliance, despite its medical or systemic causes. I found the task of challenging her health insurance company in writing for reimbursement more challenging and entertaining than the relatively simple task of fixing Emily's teeth.

Emily's case served as a reminder to me that we should never take our health for granted, or pursue Quixotic, untested treatments for simple disorders. Not long after this last visit, poor Emily died of complications of pneumonia, as she became unable to clear her lungs with her flimsy diaphragm and intercostals muscles. She was thirty.

# Allan Joins Life's Army

*What is home without a mother?*

– Alice Hawthorne

Jane was a single mom struggling to rear her only child, Allen, without any contact or help from the boy's long-departed father. Jane and Allen were referred to our dental office by her internist who had an office down the hall from our office. He had attracted many unusual people to his practice because he was often heard on the radio as "Doc" for a local A.M. radio channel.

I found Allan, now a teenager, to be a gracious, polite, well-groomed kid. Jane didn't volunteer much about herself unless you asked her directly, and it was painful hard trying to get to know her well. She was so obviously reluctant to share personal information about her past with us that we refrained from prying into that part of her life. She had devoted her whole life to her son. He was her universe, and she seemed to be interested in very little else.

Allan seemed to be a normal teenager, though he had been obsessed from an early age with anything that had to do with the military. He would always arrive in the office dressed in Army fatigues. I assumed that not having a male role model in his life gave the "manliness" of the Army a special appeal. Jane shared with us that Allan would play war games and watch any television shows that would portrayed war or combat.

I could easily sympathize, recalling that in my youth I went through a phase where I enjoyed pretending to be part of the

Rat Patrol and thought that launching dummy grenades I'd purchased from the Army Surplus store was a really "cool" thing to do. My phase was short lived, but Allan's lasted all the way through high school.

Once he'd graduated from high school a battle ensued between Allan and his mother. He wanted to join the Army at seventeen, but he needed his mother's permission. She wasn't ready to let her baby go, and the more she tried to convince him to live at home the more he wanted to leave. Allan as a teenager always had tolerated his mother's frequent bouts of depression. Yet, he craved discipline like a drug. The marketing campaign of the Army that promised " You can see the world" was the frosting on the cake. Allen had not left Minneapolis since birth.

Allen's mother had other ideas. She hoped for him to excel in school, thinking he might be able to live at home and attend college, but she had failed to motivate him academically. College was her goal, not his.

Jane knew that if she signed the permission slip for the Army she would loose the only person in her life that she cared about, and she was mentally unprepared to live day to day without his presence. Perhaps she harbored the unrealistic fantasy that he would live with her forever, remaining dependent just as he had been as a small child.

Recognizing the source of his mother's obstinacy, Allen asserted that if Jane didn't sign the permission slip, he would wait until he was eighteen and join up anyway. And if she pushed him to that extreme, he vowed he would never come back home again. Jane continued to hope that she could change his he mind by promising him just about everything in the world.

She was desperate.

He was determined.

As his eighteenth birthday drew near the both of them had many anxious moments.

One morning a local tragedy was announced on the news: "Mother shoots her teenage son and then shoots herself." Neither names nor possible motive was revealed, only the age, sex, and their relationship.

I found out later from the physician across the hall that Jane had proved herself incapable of letting Allan go. Decided that they would leave this earth together, she stole a handgun from her brother, waited one evening until he had fallen asleep, quietly walked into his room, pointed the gun at his heart and pulled the trigger. She then proceeded to put the gun up to her head and shoot herself.

Fortunately, Jane missed Allan's heart and lungs, merely injuring his shoulder. He would recover, at least physically. But would he ever be able to recover mentally from such trauma?

THE TIME I SPENT WITH Allan and Jane haunts me even today, reinforcing my belief that our goal, as parents, should be to create relationships of trust and respect with our children, while nurturing their own independence and self-confidence. We "should" want our kids to grow up, leave the nest, and fly.

As a parent I can readily understand the temptation to smother our children, and the desire to keep them close to us at all times. As Allen's case makes clear, such impulses need to be resisted. I can remember my own mother lamenting when I left town for college and how I had admired her for reluctantly encouraging me to leave. Even though I sensed she wanted me to stay near home, she also knew deep down that I needed to leave the nest.

I have come to appreciate that people who have severe mental challenges are capable of unthinkable acts. Hopefully Allan can blame her illness, and continue to love and understand the mother that cared for him for all those years.

# SHEER GOOD HUMOR

## Standing Ovation

*The best and most beautiful things in the world cannot be seen, nor touched ... but are felt in the heart.*

– Helen Keller

I was preparing a tooth for a new gold crown during my dental school clinical requirements and felt in the zone. I had carefully sculpted the patient's mouth with the perfect crown preparation in mind, a design I'd seen pictured in text books. The taper was barely more than six degrees as desired, and I'd succeeded in preserving the maximum amount of tooth structure. Swelling with pride at my own talent, I confidently awaited the approbation of my clinical instructor.

He looked into my patient's mouth, thoroughly inspecting the tooth with high-powered magnification loupes, tilting the mirror in several different angles. At last, he told the patient, "That is the most perfect crown preparation I've seen in years. Dr. Foy has really done you a great service."

My pride and ego soared. I completed the impression and cemented the temporary crown. After my patient left, the instructor came over and said, "That was a nice job. But when you're out in the real world don't expect a standing ovation from your patients. Most people value quickness and lack of pain, not line angles and perfect margins. They'll never see or appreciate that type of quality. You'll have to motivate yourself to continue to maintain it, and break your own arm slapping yourself on the back."

One of my patients, a maintenance man in his early sixties, had volunteered to go with a group of medical missionaries to the poor areas of Guyana, Africa. Larry had a full head of wavy hair, snow-white with age, and the Guyanese people exalted him as possessing great powers, looking up to him in a godlike manner.

During his stay he met and married a young African woman named Lily. My dental journey with her was one of the most surprising and gratifying of my career.

Our American emphasis on personal esthetics can seem excessive to someone from an impoverished country. Larry's new bride had a hard time adapting. She was extremely self-conscious, but at least she could speak a little English.

As with many immigrants Lily had had little or no previous dental care, and her teeth were free of fillings. I treated some minor gum disease and instructed her on proper oral hygiene techniques. Once she'd mastered a self-care routine, we were able to restore minor decay. In the beginning we were simply trying to build the foundation for cosmetic dental care. Lily was compliant and eager to fix her anterior teeth.

She'd grown up in an area of Africa where the water supply was so rich with fluoride that people often developed severe fluorosis—a condition that caused their teeth to turn reddish-brown. In her home country Lily didn't stand out, but the prevalence of white teeth in the United States made Lily ashamed of her smile. She covered her mouth when she spoke, and this was crippling her ability to adapt. Larry asked for our help.

After a consultation, Lily decided to cosmetically enhance her smile. Diagnostic casts were made to plan for size, function and space management. Despite all the discussions and pre-planning, it was still difficult for her to completely appreciate and comprehend the result.

The day of final delivery was one I'll never forget. Local anesthetic was used and Lily was cooperative throughout the procedure. When everything was cemented, cleaned and polished, I handed her a mirror. At first, she remained expressionless, and tears began to roll down her face.

I was confused by her reaction. Were these tears of joy, tears of shock or disappointment? I waited nervously for her to voice an opinion.

Lily remained stoic as she peered into the mirror. Suddenly her face lit up with a beautiful grin. She leaped out of the chair and started doing a little jig, dancing in circles around the small room. Then she dropped down on her knees and began kissing my feet.

I quickly bent over, grabbing her arms, trying to lift her up, protesting, "No, no, no, no, no...." At that moment Larry walked into the room.

It's odd to have a husband witnessing his wife on her knees kissing your shoes.

Larry laughed, and as Lily jumped up and showed him her new teeth, he exclaimed, "Wow! I can't believe it." She shrieked and ran into the waiting room, going from chair to chair to show her new smile.

Some things are better than a standing ovation.

# Mankato Mary

*Once you wake up and smell the coffee,*
*it's hard to go back to sleep.*

– Fran Dresher

Mankato Mary's visits illustrate the trials, the joys, and the challenges that are daily gifts to anyone who practices dentistry. A fastidious, middle-aged lady, Mary was confined to a wheelchair as a result of a spinal-cord injury she'd received in an automobile accident. Her wheelchair was much wider than the standard model, and she was unable to locate a dental office in southern Minnesota with both the expertise required to manage her current medical complications and doors wide enough to accommodate her wheelchair. Therefore, her rehabilitation center referred her to us.

Mary visited us on a number of occasions, and we soon came to know what to expect. She would make the ninety-mile trip north from her home in a small town south of Mankato, accompanied by her small dog, a personal attendant, and a van driver. For a normal recall appointment we would schedule her for a one-hour hygiene appointment and an additional hour for any dental work she might need, to save her the inconvenience of making a second trip. If work was not required I'd simply take a long lunch.

On one occasion Mary was scheduled for a 10:00 AM appointment with the hygienist and an 11:00 AM with me. Ten o'clock came and left, but no sign of Mary. About twenty-five minutes after the hour the phone rang. It was Mary calling from the second floor of our building. They had parked their van in the ramp which is connected to our building by a skyway. As they were wheeling around a corner her "Foley catheter bag" got caught on something and it ripped open, spilling urine all over the place. She was now down at the pharmacy where they were trying to put everything back together. She asked if we could still see her that morning. We still had ninety minutes reserved for her, and told her we would have no difficulty addressing her dental needs within that time frame. Life is unpredictable sometimes, but flexibility was our mantra.

I had planned to eat lunch in the doctor's lounge at the hospital that day, and took the elevator down to the second floor to access the skyway. As the elevator door opened I noticed the building manager and the building's owner pass by, also headed for the skyway. I followed them down the hall until they stopped in front of a large wet spot on the carpet. The building manager immediately bent over and dabbed his bare pointer finger into the wet area. Then, rising, he gave his finger a sniff. "Coffee," he blurted out.

I couldn't contain myself, and as I passed them I remarked, smiling, "Well, it may have started out that way."

They gave me a bewildered look as I continued by them, and I paused to share the tale of Mary's mishap.

The visual of the finger sniff test continued to tickle my funny bones, and as I entered the doctor's lounge my face was beaming with delight. One of the doctors noticed the amusement radiating from my face and said, "Whatever you're on, I want some of it."

# Forgotten Perfection

*We read the world wrong and say that it deceives us.*

– Rabindranath Tagore

Many of the hospital charts I've read of patients from the Psych Unit over the years have histories that are hair-raising scary and all but unbelievable. There are many people who have heard voices, often telling them to harm themselves or others. Many people have experienced terrible things and are struggling simply to keep on living in their mentally troubled world.

A numbers of patients who bear the curse of a mental disorder conclude that an evil force of some type is involved. Some believe they are evil themselves, or even the "devil" incarnate. Others believe they're possessed by evil, or that the devil communicates with them. No doubt this is a way for them to explain their disruptive thought patterns. Suicide often looms as an escape from such torments.

One patient—I'll call him John—thought he was Damian, the son of the devil. He had a mouth full of rampant decay due to both an excessive intake of soda pop and the side-effect of the psychotropic medications he was taking, which inhibited his salivary flow. Our plan was to restore his teeth while he was in the hospital during several extended appointments spread across several weeks. He was civil to me, but he would follow my female staff members with staring, lustful eyes. They said that his glare made them feel creepy. I would never leave them alone in the room with him. Many of his comments were completely inappropriate and he would laugh at the strangest things.

One Sunday morning when our office was closed, he called my personal residence and got my answering machine. He left a blood-curdling howl on my machine. "It's John. I suppose, doctor, you're in church, ha ha ha!" My wife heard the message and was terrified not only by the tone, but also by the fact that this guy could get our home phone number.

After years of seeing patients who had been hospitalized for mental health problems, I'm convinced that most of them need intensive treatment, including a juggling of their pharmacological management. While in the hospital they would get their mental attitude adjusted and also receive help finding outside community support. With the help of these elements of treatment their day-to-day functions would stabilize…until the next mental crisis or crash.

One day I ran into one of the "shrinks" that refers patients to our office for dental problems, and I asked him, "Over the last twenty-five years of seeing your patients, I have seen many devils and people possessed by the devil, but I have yet to see someone who thinks they are Jesus Christ." He looked up at me with contempt and smiled, then he said, "Jesus has been over there, but Pat, you should know better. Jesus does not have cavities."

Coping with the ills of mankind can be trying at times, but it demands that you develop a means of dealing with the daily grind. There is a undercurrent of medical humor that can be perceived as perverse, but it provides an outlet that can help you maintain your own mental health.

# Cultural Gifts

*What one has not experienced,*
*one will never understand in print.*
– Isadora Duncan

The summer day we picked for our office "boat day" turned out to be one of the most unforgettable days in my professional career.

It was a sunny day, hot and humid, with very little wind. The pristine blue sky reflected joyously across the massive water of Lake Minnetonka, graciously welcoming us into its myriad bays, all similar yet each in some way unique.

Knowing that it was going to be hot, everyone dressed and packed appropriately—everyone except Sadia. Sadia had worked part-time as my chairside dental assistant for six years. She was from Somalia, a practicing Muslim, and at all times she wore a burka and a long dress which covered every inch of her body. In our dental office she remained covered, and on our "boat day," while the rest of us lounged in summer shorts or swim suits, Sadia chose to retain her traditional mode of dress.

That morning we aimlessly motored around the big lake, sight-seeing and attempted to staying cool. As lunchtime approached, we decided to motor over to Lord Fletchers, a large restaurant with plenty of moorings for boaters and ample outdoor seating.

Fletchers had a good lunch time crowd that day, as usual, and we received a good many unabashed stares as we walked down the dock—a fifty-year-old man in shorts accompanied by four women, one black and dressed with a burka, another in a bikini top and shorts, and the other two in shorts and short sleeved shirts. Such as entourage is not commonly seen in the western suburbs of Minneapolis.

The Foy Harem had arrived. The lunch was relaxed and delightful. As we leisurely ate our lunch the temperature continued to climb.

After lunch we motored through a couple of intimate channels and we were progressing slowly with no relief from the wind. It had become almost unbearably steamy, and one of the ladies suggested we go for a swim. We stopped the boat near the Neurenberg Gardens and dropped anchor. I threw a couple of inflatable tubes and some floating toys overboard for buoyancy. Stacey and Jan went in the water immediately, though Betty (a non-swimmer) would only hang her feet into the water. I jumped in only to cool off and climbed back into the boat almost immediately. Sadia appeared to be miserably cooking buried in her black, multi-layered dress and matching head cover. As the sweat beaded up on her forehead, Stacey and Jan began to encourage her to come into the water herself.

Sadia had grown up in Kenya, and she shared with us that she had only gone swimming once in her life, on a remote African river. As a child she had listened to the tragic stories of children lost or eaten in the rivers, and the children were generally allowed to swim only when there was vigilant supervision. The one day she had actually gone for a swim, men were posted upstream and downstream to stand watch for predators such as alligators. So when she was asked to come into the lake, her first concern was to know what type of creatures that might be lurking in the waters?

"Are there sharks, alligators, snakes?" Sadia asked.

"No," we all replied. We assured her there are no animals, snakes, sharks, or anything that would harm her.

"I do not know how to swim and I have my dress on," She retorted, hoping we'd stop our verbal barrage. "We have life vests that will keep you afloat and the dress can get wet." We all reassured her. So, with help from the ladies, Sadia shed a layer or two of clothing and donned a life vest.

She first put her toe in the water with a great deal of trepidation and then shyly looked around to see if we were watching. She smiled and then hung down her face in timid embarrassment. We continued to encouraged her, assuring her repeatedly that she would be OK. As she continued to inch her way down the ladder, we could see the mounting anxiety on her face, but also something else. The fresh coolness of the water came as welcome relief from the heat. Sadia descended the ladder until finally she was in the water up to her shoulders. Slowly the look of panic melted away and the pure look of joy beamed brightly from her burka-wrapped face. I have never seen such a transformation from terror to ecstasy in such a short time. All of us to this day treasure witnessing her bravery and unbridled glee as, putting her unquestioning trust in our encouragement, she entered the unfamiliar waters of bass-infested Lake Minnetonka.

Sadia tested the buoyancy of the life vest again and again before finally letting go of the ladder. After floating in total amazement for a few seconds, she slowly inched away from the ladder for short periods at a time, bobbing in the water and smiling like a child touching snow for the first time. Returning to the ladder, she dipped her head, still wrapped in her burka, backwards into the water. As the burka absorbed the water in grew heavier and eventually slipped off her head completely.

Though I had worked side by side with Sadia for more than six years, up until that moment I had never seen a single hair on her head. It wasn't a big deal to me, but it was to her, due to her cultural and religious traditions. At first, she looked at me as if

I had violated her in some strange way, but almost immediately she accepted the unintended breach. The burka remained off while she plunged into the coolness of the lake's relief.

Sadia's comfort level grew as the afternoon progressed. She started to climb into and out of the tubes. We were witnessing the pure joy of human discovery. It was clear to all of us that we were sharing a precious moment that we'd treasure forever. Seeing Sadia's hair wasn't important to me, but seeing her experience the novelty of the water for the first time in her adult life was unforgettably spiritual.

As the boating event came to an end, Sadia re-wrapped her Burka, we docked, returned to our cars and went our separate ways. The next Monday, Sadia came up to me in the lab and thanked me for the boat ride. She confessed that she'd told her family she had sinned, but she had a good time. In her culture, for a married woman to show her hair to another man is considered unholy, but it was not practical to do otherwise while trying to swim in the lake. As is so often the case, regardless of the religion, righteousness and having a good time seldom seem to go together.

# Tough Love for a Sailboat Racer

*Red sky in the morning, a sailor's warning.*
*Red sky at night, a sailor's delight.*

– ancient weather adage

In the heat of battle during our weekly sailboat race on Lake Minnetonka, the western sky grew dark and bubbled up with the threat of an evening summer squall.

The wind dropped suddenly and more than a hundred sailboats were stalled in dead air, parked in the middle of the lake. Greenish-black clouds billowed near the ground, while white puffs of clouds shot high up into eternity.

The solemn silence that filled the lake was suddenly punctuated by the ring of my cell phone.

"Are you still sailing?" my wife, Lynne, demanded.

"Yes, we're still sailing," I responded patiently.

"Well, I'm watching the weather radar on television and they say a storm is heading right for Lake Minnetonka."

I confidently replied, "The clouds seem to be skirting south of us. The committee boat has a weather radio on board and they haven't cancelled the race yet."

"Listen, I'm pregnant and here at home with a two-and-a-half-year old. If you die on that damn lake, I am not going to your funeral!" She hung up.

I turned to my crew, "Lynne says those clouds are heading right at us. We're in third place and dead in the water. Should we bail?" After a short debate, we dropped the sails and threw on the motor.

The roar echoed across the silent lake and drew attention to our conspicuous retreat. Not one other boat followed as we quickly navigated back to shore. The fleet remained stuck in the calm, waiting for a sign of salvation from the race committee.

We motored back to the yacht club, tucked away our sails, locked up the boat and sought shelter under the roof of the outside patio.

Suddenly, we heard the "boom, boom, boom" of cannon fire reverberating from the committee boat, signaling the race had been cancelled. Sails quickly dropped and there was a mad dash to beat the storm.

Most of the crews were hit by violent winds and rain, stranding the small-keel boats. Black clouds rumbled above and explosive bolts of lightning darted unpredictably around the shoreline.

That night, many a drenched man sought the secret of my wisdom. I was the smartest sailor on Lake Minnetonka.

Thank you, Lynne!

# Mrs. Olson

*When the solution is simple, God is answering.*

– Albert Einstein

Mrs. Olson lived well into her nineties and valued her dental health. Her intuition and attention was a lesson to us all that living healthy takes a mental attitude and desire.

One day while she was seated in the dental chair, I walked over to the sink and took a drink of water. She gasped and said in her strong Swedish accent, "Doctor, you drink that water?"

"Yes, when my throat is dry, I need to drink water."

"All the chemicals the city puts in that water, that water will kill you," she warned. " I buy bottled water, but that is getting too expensive. So, I mix the city water with the bottled water. Now I will die half as fast."

My first reaction was amusement, but who am I to laugh at someone who is a healthy ninety-plus? One reason she has lived so long could be her prudent concern for what she ingests into her body.

One winter day Mrs. Olson had an appointment for a dental restoration and was seated in an operatory that tends to be colder than the rest of our office.

"Doctor," she said, "I feel a draft. Is there a window open?" In our building the windows are permanently fixed to the concrete frame and cannot be moved.

"No, Mrs. Olson, we cannot open these windows."

"You get a man," she replied confidently, "and he'll open the window for you."

13449818R00089

Made in the USA
Charleston, SC
11 July 2012